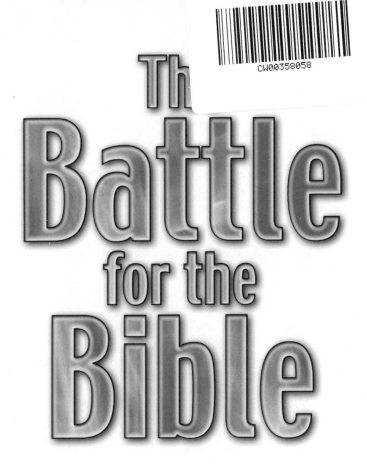

The Battle for the Bible

by David Marshall

© David Marshall. 2004
The Battle for the Bible is a revised and updated edition of
The Battle for the Book, first published in 1991
by Autumn House.

Cover photography Joe Partridge/REX FEATURES

Copyright © 2004
First published in 2004
Reprinted in 2005

British Library Cataloguing in Publication Data.
A catalogue record for this book is available
from the British Library.

ISBN 1 903921 23 6

*Published by
Autumn House, Grantham, England
Printed in Thailand*

The Battle for the Bible

by David Marshall

The story of how the Bible was written,
who wrote it, and when.

The story of how the sixty-six books of the Bible came to be
regarded as special and were brought together.

The story of how the Bible survived the centuries and how
battle after battle was fought over its accuracy and,
under remarkable circumstances, won.

The story of how astonishing manuscripts and
archaeological finds have, time after time,
proved the Bible right and the critics wrong.

The story of the English Bible through Caedmon of Whitby, King
Alfred the Great, John Wyclif, William Tyndale, the King James
Version, J. B. Phillips — to Peterson's *Message* paraphrase and
Lacey's *Street Bible.*

Contents

About the author

David Marshall has a first degree and a PhD in History from the University of Hull. His doctorate was done under the supervision of Professor John P. Kenyon (1926-1996) to whose memory this revised edition is dedicated.

Dr Marshall taught for a number of years before becoming a writer and magazine editor. He has published twenty books on historical, travel, and biblical themes. These have included *Where Jesus Walked*, *God's Good News*, *Footprints of Paul*, *Pilgrim Ways*, *New Age Versus the Gospel*, *Is God Still in the Healing Business?*, *Joy in Jesus*, *A Treasury of Christmas Gems*, and *When the Only Way Out is Through* – all published with Autumn House.

Marshall writes and edits full time, is married, and part of a large, three-tier family and lives in Lincolnshire. His hobbies include walking, steam railways, travel and photography.

The author wishes to express his profound thanks to archaeologist Dr William Shea for ensuring the accuracy of Section Four and that the narrative incorporated the most up-to-date findings.
He also owes a great debt of gratitude to the late Dr Hugh Dunton and to Miss Nan Tucker.

Introduction

The Making of the Bible

It has always been controversial.

People have been gaoled for reading it.

Men have been executed for translating it.

It has been banned and burned in countries scared of its influence. It was once described as 'the most subversive single volume in existence'. In the years of Communism a secret network existed to smuggle it under the Iron Curtain. Smugglers caught distributing it disappeared without trace.

It has been lampooned, ridiculed, denounced and shot down in flames as no other book has. The critics have attacked its factual accuracy; the characters and nations whose activities it records have been laughed off as 'mythical'. But under the fierce glare of scientific enquiry and archaeological research its assertions have been authenticated as fact. Time and time again its critics have been forced to withdraw in disarray.

The book was right. The critics were wrong.

But the critics then simply shifted their ground and began to shoot from a new angle.

Meanwhile the scholars worked on. The archaeologists continued their digging. Tablets inscribed with ancient cuneiform writing came to light. And the assertions made so dogmatically by another school of 'experts' were proved groundless. The *tells,* the ancient cities and settlements of the Middle East, seem to be rich with layer on layer of artefacts waiting to provide testimony to the book's accuracy.

Those artefacts, those tablets and parchments, together and through the tools of modern science, have at so many points verified the book that those with an open mind are obliged to entertain at least the possibility that behind it stands a divine presence.

Portions of the Bible have been translated into more than 1,710 languages. In a single year fifty million copies were produced in the United States alone. Each year an average of £4.1 million is spent in *Britain* on copies of the Bible. Apparently, £6.3 million worth are exported from Britain each year. A Bible Society spokesperson says that this amounts to a grand total of 3,466,000 copies per annum.

But statistics are misleading; and never more so than in this instance. If this ancient book is a best seller, it is not a best seller in the sense that the paperbacks of J. K. Rowling, Jilly Cooper and Frederick Forsyth are best sellers. *In fact, it's probably the world's least-read best seller.*

But, for all that, there is a strange, unaccountable fascination about it.

And why?

Is it viewed as a good luck charm?

Or is there a vague feeling that between its covers lies a wisdom that lends meaning to the journey from cradle to grave: a window on origin and destiny, time and eternity?

Is there a feeling – yes, irrational, even 'superstitious' – that the great Power behind the universe inspired the minds and experiences of the forty men who wrote this book that has proved so durable? And that, if that is the case, it may, just *may,* have something to say to *us?*

Has there been a reaction among postmoderns to the feeling that success in life is entirely to be measured by the acquisition of material possessions? To the assumption that absolute truth emerges only from laboratories? To the idea that trying to make sense of so complex and sophisticated a world is simply too much to ask?

A reaction, perhaps, to the 'modern' acceptance of the kind of 'sense' made of things by Sigmund Freud, Charles Darwin and Karl Marx? A fear that the modern 'received wisdom', in fact, poses more questions than it answers?

Am I going too far, too fast? Raising blood pressure, overheating collars?

Or are we embarrassed, uncomfortable with any suggestion that an ancient book might have something to say in the age of the silicon chip? Preposterous. Right? A fall-back to an age of superstition best forgotten. Yes?

Perhaps our world is so problem free that we are no longer in need of super-human guidance delivered through some inspired book. . . . Or perhaps life really *is* what the modern 'wise men' told us – 'a nightmare between two eternities', 'the penalty for the crime of being born'. . . . Perhaps the human race really *is* no more than 'a planetary eczema' with each member purely 'an enlarged protein molecule'. . . .

So many times the Bible – and, therefore, its explanation of the meaning of life – has been 'debunked'. And then, as if stubbornly unwilling to quit, it has made a comeback.

In the Age of Reason, Voltaire gave a lecture on it in his Paris home. He said the old book was, without question, completely obsolete and within a century of that date would be out of print, unobtainable. That was in the eighteenth century. One century on from the year in which Voltaire gave his lecture, the home in which he had given it was a centre dedicated to the distribution of the book he had written off as obsolete. His words were forgotten, but his home was used to distribute the Bible in scores of languages to the farthest reaches of the planet. Voltaire had made an unquestionable contribution to the thought and life of his age; but is it possible that the book he declared obsolete is ageless – relevant in every age?

Could this ancient book that won't quit be worth a second look? Does it really have something to say in our postmodern age? Is it worthwhile to take a second glance at the evidence unearthed in recent years for its accuracy and authenticity?

In a society like ours, in a world like ours – isn't *anything* worth a try?

1

Where the Bible came from

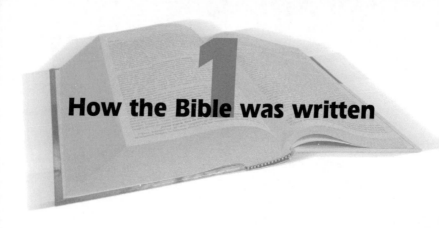

How the Bible was written

Scrolls and parchments

Paul, who wrote about two-thirds of the part of the Bible called the New Testament, fell foul of the Roman Empire. During the last winter of his life, under sentence of death, he smuggled a letter to his student Timothy. In it we find these words:

'Do your best to come to me quickly. . . . When you come, bring the cloak that I left with Carpus at Troas, and my scrolls, especially the parchments.'[1]

Paul wanted his heavy overcoat. How could a scholar concentrate on his studies in a dank, below-ground-level Roman dungeon?

To have his scrolls and parchments to hand was even more vital.

Following the conquests of Alexander the Great, after 336BC, the world had been Hellenised. Everyone who was anyone spoke the *Koine*, the Greek dialect common to all countries. Paul was no exception. Hence the word he used for cloak was *phailones*; the word for scrolls was *biblion*; and the word for parchments, *membrana*.

The Greek words for scrolls and parchments reflected the material from which they were made.

A *biblion* was a reed-plant which grew on river banks. The inner leaf or bark of this plant was dried in strips, and rows of the dried strips – criss-cross fashion – were gummed together to make a writing material.

The Greek word *membrana* was actually borrowed from Latin and means 'membrane'. This was part of an animal skin also processed for use as a writing material.

But in tracing the origin of the word Bible, *biblion* is the clue. Among the alternative names for the plant from which it was made was *byblos*. This name was given by the Greeks to a town in Phoenicia: Byblos.

When referring to the Old and New Testaments, Greek-speaking Christians use the words *ta biblia*, 'the books'. Latin-speaking Christians came to use the two testaments as one book and called it *Biblia* (treating it as a singular noun).

Hence the English word, Bible.[2]

The languages of the Bible

Having discovered where the word Bible came from we have also found out what many of the sixty-six books that make up the Bible were written on. Either a criss-cross of dried reed bark or treated animal skins. In addition to these, however, further back into the Old Testament, other writing materials were used, including clay or wooden tablets, chips of limestone or broken pieces of pottery.

Now other questions have to be answered. Among them are: In what language were the books of the Bible written? Who wrote them? And when?

Hebrew

Sabra literally means 'cactus flower'. These days, however, it is the term used in Israel for the secularly minded young Israelis born in Israel who work the *kibbutzim* (fortified villages based around farming but including some industries and crafts).

Sabras are commonly employed by archaeologists in their digs in Israel. Typically, *kibbutzim* contain no synagogues and are entirely Hebrew-speaking.

Recently an archaeologist was discussing Deuteronomy (the fifth of the Bible's sixty-six books) with a visitor. He had an ancient fragment of *biblion* with a chapter or two written in the Hebrew in which the bulk of the Old Testament was set down.

'*Ivrit*, or modern Hebrew,' the archaeologist was saying, 'represents a revival of ancient Hebrew carried out in the early years of the twentieth century by Ben Yehuda. But it is near enough to the original language to enable anyone who reads it to read the ancient Hebrew of the Bible.'

'If that is so,' replied the visitor with some disbelief, 'call the *sabra* working over there and ask her to read your fragment of Deuteronomy. Although she has no religious education she should be able to manage it if what you say is true.'

The sun-bronzed *sabra* was called over. She read every word of the ancient fragment without faltering.

The language of the Old Testament is Hebrew. Despite the hundreds of years over which it was written the linguistic differences between the earlier and later writings are few and of no importance. Today any educated Israeli can read his holy book in its original written-down form.

Aramaic

A few sections of the Old Testament were written in Aramaic. These include some chapters in Ezra and Daniel and one verse in Jeremiah. The Aramaic language is closely related to Hebrew.

Aramaic was the language of certain Aramean tribes who migrated from Mesopotamia – between the Tigris and Euphrates rivers – to Syria. In the eight century BC the Assyrians forcibly deported Arameans to all provinces of their vast empire, thus disseminating the Aramaic language over a wide area.

That certain sections of the Old Testament were written in Aramaic is accounted for by the fact that through the wholesale deportation of Arameans the Assyrians had made Aramaic an international language. Hundreds of Aramaic documents from the times of Ezra and Daniel have been found in the Middle East.

In the centuries immediately before the birth of Jesus, Aramaic had replaced Hebrew as the language of conversation among the Jews. Nevertheless, when the rabbi read the scrolls and parchments in the synagogue, he read them in Hebrew.

The four New Testament accounts of the life of Jesus indicate that though he *read* Hebrew he *spoke* Aramaic. In a number of cases fragments from the Aramaic conversation of Jesus were retained in the Greek New Testament. In the story of the raising of Jairus's daughter, for example, Jesus said the words, 'Little girl, get up,' in Aramaic: '*Talitha cumi*'.[3]

Greek

The tiny spurts of Aramaic are the exception. The New Testament was written in Greek: the *Koine*. A Greek (or a Hellene, the name by which he called himself) was a man whose language and culture was Greek; and Greece (or Hellas, the name he used) extended as far as the Greek language and culture did. The *koine dialektos* was the common speech of the Greek community. It drew on several ancient dialects, especially the dialect of Athens (Attic).

Before Palestine had become part of the Roman Empire, as it was at the time of Jesus, it had been conquered by Alexander the Great. It was then that the Greek language and culture began to take hold. After Alexander's death the eastern portion of his empire was divided between his generals: Ptolemy took Egypt and Palestine; Seleuces took from Thrace to India.

The first Jews to become Hellenised were those who settled in the new city of Alexandria during the rule of Ptolemy. It is likely that it was during this period that the Jewish trading classes and the upper classes of Judaea itself began to speak the *koine*.

It was, however, the Seleucid kings Antiochus III and IV who *enforced* Greek language and culture. The Seleucid capital, Antioch, became a great centre for Greek sport, theatre and pageantry. The extension of the Seleucid Empire to include Palestine provoked a reaction among the Jews.

Two parties emerged, one supporting, one opposing Greek ways. Welcomed by the liberals, the Seleucid tyrant Antiochus IV entered Jerusalem in 171BC. He outraged the conservatives and provoked the Revolt of the Maccabees by plundering and desecrating the temple.

But the culture and language for which the Seleucids had stood had bitten deep into Palestine. The language and aspects of the culture outlived the revolts of the period and the occupation by the Romans. Indeed, Caesar Augustus, who presided over the Roman world in the year Jesus was born, was determined to unite it through the diffusion of Greek culture.

The Roman Empire was in fact bilingual. In the Roman army Latin was the official language, but, for the rest, Greek remained the official tongue in the eastern Mediterranean lands. In Rome itself Greek was spoken as much as Latin.

For centuries it appeared that the form of Greek in which the New Testament was written was not only peculiar, but exclusive. Aware that its forms could not be found elsewhere, some sarcastically called it 'the language of the Holy Ghost'. Since the 1880s, however, scraps of papyrus and pieces of pottery have been discovered in the Near East, more especially in Egypt. These documents and artefacts have been found to contain 'vernacular Greek', strikingly similar to the Greek of the New Testament. Hence, while New Testament Greek is very dissimilar to the classical Greek spoken and written in *earlier* centuries, it has been proven beyond doubt to be the form of Greek spoken and written in the *first* century AD, the international language most widely understood: the *koine*.

The very popularity of the form of Greek in which the New Testament was written helps to explain the spread of Christianity in the first century. It was the most thoroughly international language. Hence it was the language most appropriate for the propagation of the vital new message calculated to 'turn the world upside down'.

References:
[1] 2 Timothy 4:9, 13.
[2] F. F. Bruce, *The Books and the Parchments*, pages 2-6.
[3] Mark 5:41; 7:34; 15:34.

Note

A Greek version of the Old Testament called the *Septuagint* (from the Latin for seventy) existed at the time of Jesus.

Ptolemy, building massive libraries, made Alexandria a great centre of scholarship. He invited the Jerusalem high priest, Eleazar, to appoint scholars to translate the Scriptures (the Old Testament, that is) from Hebrew to Greek. Six translators were chosen from each of the twelve tribes of Israel. They went to Alexandria with an especially accurate version of the Torah (the Jewish Scriptures).

It was from the fact that seventy-two men were involved in the work of translation that the name 'Septuagint' was derived.

By the time of Jesus a million Jews lived in Alexandria. They forgot both Hebrew and Aramaic and read the *Torah* in its Greek version. But it was to the Christians, not the Jews, that we owe almost all of the manuscript copies of the Septuagint that have survived to our own day. From the first century AD Christians adopted it as their 'authorised version' of the Old Testament.

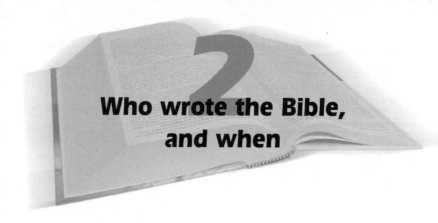

Who wrote the Bible, and when

Forty men wrote the sixty-six books of the Bible. They did so over approximately 1,600 years.

In the fifteenth century before Christ, Moses, in exceptional circumstances, led the Hebrews out of slavery in Egypt.*

Moses, the author

Moses lived to the age of 120. His life divides into three periods of forty years each.

Born a Hebrew, he was, nevertheless, brought up at the Egyptian court where, for his first forty years, he gained both political and military experience, as well as the best education available in his time.

Abruptly, Moses was forced to flee into exile after an ill-judged (and violent) attack upon an Egyptian, provoked by his sympathy for the enslaved Hebrews, his own people. He spent the second forty-year period working as a wilderness shepherd in Midian.

It was after that that he assumed the role of the great liberator of his people.

Preacher Dwight Moody said: 'The first forty years of Moses' life he was becoming a somebody. The second forty years of his life he was becoming a nobody. And the third forty years of his life he was proving to the world what God can do with somebody who is a nobody.'

In fact, it is likely that Moses accomplished more in the middle phase of his life than learning how to be a nobody and tending sheep in the desert.

When, following Moses' death, Joshua led the Hebrews into the land west of the Jordan, it was with God's admonition, '*Do not let this Book of the Law depart from your mouth.*' Soon he was gathering his migrant nation together. Half of them swarmed over the slopes of Mount Gerazim, half over Mount Ebal. There '*Joshua read all the words of the Law . . . just as it is written in the Book of the Law. There was not a word of all that Moses had commanded that Joshua did not read to the whole assembly of Israel.*' Much later Joshua was still exhorting the people '*to obey all that is written in the Book of . . . Moses.*'[1]

The Books of Moses are accepted as being the *Torah* or *Pentateuch*, the first five books of the Old Testament (Genesis, Exodus, Leviticus, Numbers and Deuteronomy). No one is saying that Moses was the only author of the Torah or Pentateuch. Nevertheless, King David, whose reign began *circa* 1050BC (that is, 500 years or so *after* Moses), accepted that he was the principal author of the five books.[2] Between the golden age of empire under David and Solomon and the destruction of Jerusalem by the Babylonians in 586BC, two other kings — Amaziah and Josiah — (by implication) accepted Moses' authorship.[3]

The first of his five books — Genesis — Moses would appear to have part written, part collated, during the middle period of his life, the period in Midian.

Exodus extends the narrative begun in Genesis. In certain statements Moses is specifically named as having been the author of it. The activities of Moses as a chronicler, as well as a lawgiver and a codifier of law, are actually mentioned.[4] The skills used by Moses in authoring Exodus, Numbers, Leviticus and Deuteronomy in the third period of his life had almost certainly been acquired during the higher education of Egypt to which he had been exposed in the first period of his life.[5] Jesus accepted that Moses had written Exodus.[6] Leviticus is the core of what Jesus called 'the law of Moses'.[7] Elsewhere he implied that Moses had been a prolific writer.[8]

The fifth book of the Pentateuch, Deuteronomy, was clearly edited and added to since it incorporates the story of Moses' own death! Nevertheless, Jesus and the early Christian leaders, by their words and the use they made of it, clearly accepted Moses as the main author of Deuteronomy.[9]

There is a tradition in both Christianity and Judaism that Moses also authored the profoundly reflective and beautifully poetical book of Job. And, further, that he did so during the middle (Midianite) period of his life. *Par excellence* Job is the book that grapples with the problem, Why is there pain, disease and death in a world over which an all-powerful, all-loving God presides? If the author of Job was indeed Moses, he was using Job's story to answer the question, How can my people be exploited as slaves in Egypt and God still be God? Through the various 'speakers' in the Book, Moses is exploring alternative views of the nature of God, and reaching the 'loving, merciful' model to which most Jews and Christians adhere. The theological framework of Job leans on Genesis with its account of the Fall, the origin of evil, and its depiction of a personal, malevolent devil.

Unity and diversity

Even if you accept that only, say, a part of *one* of the six books attributed to Moses was actually written by him, you have accepted that the Bible began to be written 3,500 years ago. And, since there can be little doubt that the last book of the New Testament was written around the end of the first century AD, you have also accepted that the Bible was 1,600 years in the writing. Having accepted that, you cannot but marvel at the unity of thought, narrative and revelation. Marvel, too, at the absence of conflict among the messages written by forty different individuals, from an immense diversity of backgrounds, education, historical periods and geographical locations.

Consider the diversity of occupation among the men who wrote the Bible.

A general. The narrative of the book of Joshua, though written in the third person, is widely accepted as having been written by Joshua himself. This does not exclude the possibility of additions after his death, or that Joshua collated part of the narrative and actually wrote other parts. Joshua was a general.

A priest. It is conjectured that the book of Judges was written by Samuel, and fairly generally accepted that the first twenty-four chapters of the first book of Samuel were written by Samuel. Samuel was a priest.

A scribe. The remainder of the books of Samuel were written by Nathan and Gad (see 1 Chronicles 29:29). These men were prophets and scribes.

The historical narratives of the two books of Kings and the two books of Chronicles represent the compilation of a variety of historical sources, but it is impossible to tell who undertook this painstaking task for the book of Kings. However, insofar as the two books of Chronicles, Ezra and Nehemiah are closely related to one another in language, style and general points of view, it may be assumed that there was one author. The fact that Chronicles ends in the middle of a sentence which is completed in the opening verses of Ezra may indicate that Ezra was the author. Similarly there is a close relationship between the books of Ezra and Nehemiah; the ancients saw them as one book, not two. Evidence in the books themselves suggests that they were written, or at the very least completed, in the period of the Persian domination, *circa* 400BC. The author, Ezra, was a priest of a priestly family.

A king. The book of Psalms is the hymnbook of the Bible. Hence there is a great diversity of authors. Most notable among them was David, a shepherd who became a king.

Internal evidence in the book of Proverbs identifies King Solomon as its author. There is little doubt that Solomon also wrote Ecclesiastes and the book known as the Song of Solomon. Solomon was a king-scholar.

Prophets, slaves, herdsmen – and a prime minister. Some of the prophetic books of the Old Testament were written by 'professional' prophets. Isaiah was an educated Hebrew aristocrat of the royal line; and he might well have been helped by others. Jeremiah certainly had the assistance of his trusted secretary, Baruch.

The long, intricate, and, at times, puzzling book of Ezekiel was written by a (highly educated) Hebrew slave working as part of a slave gang in the mud flats of the plains of Babylon near the

Kebah Canal. Hence the Bible can be said to count among its contributors a slave.

The book of Daniel, by contrast, is believed by many to have been written by the man who bears its name, a man who, in turn, served Babylonian and Persian kings in the position of first minister.

Among the 'minor prophets' is Hosea, a 'professional' prophet, though a rather exceptional one: he filled the prophetic office for a period in excess of seventy years. Joel is also simply known as a prophet. Amos is designated a herdsman and a gatherer of sycamore figs. Despite a mention in the book of Kings, nothing is known about Jonah's occupation. Micah was a younger contemporary of Isaiah, but we do not know his occupation. Zephaniah had a royal heredity; he was descended from Hezekiah. Zechariah was probably a priest.

When Malachi, the last prophet of the Old Testament, came to deliver his message, the period of the exile was a distant memory. Malachi set down his message *circa* 425BC. Many commentators conjecture that he was a priest.

The four gospel writers. The New Testament contains a similar diversity of authors. The gospel writers – Matthew, Mark, Luke and John – were, respectively, an officer of the Inland Revenue, an early Christian eager to set down the recollections of his elders, a physician, and the mystical, well-loved disciple of Jesus.

A tentmaker – and an intellectual. Paul, who wrote most of the letters contained in the New Testament, was a tentmaker by trade. In addition, however, he was a theologian, an intellectual and, prior to his conversion to Christianity, one of the leaders of the Jews.

Peter, the fisherman – and writer. By contrast Peter was a fisherman. The author of the letter of James might well have been a brother of Jesus himself.

A motley collection to produce so many books with such great diversity of style but with equally great uniformity of message and purpose.

When were the gospels written?

Of the four gospels, Mark's, most would agree, was written first. How can we know that?

Because, as we read the first three gospels, it becomes clear that Matthew and Luke borrowed heavily from Mark. Some stories are told in exactly the same words; the teaching of Jesus is presented in an almost identical way. Mark can be divided into 105 sections. Of these, ninety-three occur in Matthew, and eighty-one in Luke. Only four are not included in either Matthew or Luke. Mark has 661 verses; Matthew has 1,068 verses; Luke has 1,149 verses. Of Mark's 661 verses, Matthew reproduces no fewer than 606. Occasionally he alters the wording slightly; but he reproduces 51% of Mark's actual words. Of Mark's 661 verses, Luke reproduces 320, and 53% of Mark's actual words. Of the fifty-five verses of Mark which Matthew does not reproduce, thirty-one are found in Luke. Hence there are only twenty-four verses in Mark which do not occur in Matthew and Luke.

Obviously Matthew and Luke were based on Mark, and Mark was the first of the gospels.

Hence Mark is the 'essential gospel'; Matthew and Luke even followed Mark's order of events. There is a fast pace and a gripping realism in Mark. Over and over again he includes vivid details in his narrative; evidence that Mark was basing his narrative on an eye-witness account – almost certainly that of Peter.

The fact that Matthew, Mark and Luke have so much in common has led scholars to refer to them as the 'Synoptic Gospels'. (*Synoptic* comes from the Greek words which mean 'to see together'.)

The 'Q' source. There are, however, 200 additional verses in Matthew and Luke not present in Mark. These are concerned with what Jesus *said*, whereas the main preoccupation of Mark was with what Jesus *did*. Scholars have assumed that Matthew and Luke had recourse to another source book in addition to Mark. They have called it Q (short for *Quelle*, the German word for *source*). The other source – Q – was clearly a book of the sayings of Jesus. Beyond that, no one knows anything about it or has ever been able to find it.

The gospel for the Jews. Matthew's gospel is essentially the gospel written to convince the Jews that Jesus is the Messiah. Matthew eagerly demonstrates that all of the prophecies of the

Old Testament were fulfilled in Jesus and that, therefore, *he must be* the Messiah. Matthew's gospel is also preoccupied with the relationship between Jesus and the Jews, whether positive or negative.

The gospel for the Gentiles. Luke's gospel was essentially a gospel written for the Gentiles. He demonstrates tremendous care in setting out the events of the gospel narrative in the context of secular history. To pinpoint the year of Jesus' birth, Luke names the key ruling figures: Caesar Augustus; Quirinius, governor of Syria; and Herod, king of Judea. Luke is even more careful to date the emergence of John the Baptist (Luke 3:1, 2).

The intimate gospel. John's gospel is very different from the other three. When John's gospel was written it is clear that the gospels of Matthew, Mark and Luke were already available. Perhaps John, the disciple who had been closest to Jesus, read the other gospel accounts in his old age and thought that before it was too late he had to set down on paper his own specific, intimate recollections of the life and teaching of Jesus.

John omits much of what Matthew, Mark and Luke had already set down. What was the point of repeating it? But he knew that there was much that they had omitted. And *that* he was eager to include. Only John tells of the marriage feast at Cana, the introduction of the new birth teaching to Nicodemus, of the woman of Samaria, of the raising of Lazarus, of the way Jesus washed his disciples' feet, and of the wonderful 'Upper Room Sermon' of John 13-17.

In John's gospel each disciple assumes a personality of his own; John had known them all well. Of course, in informing Mark, Peter had known them equally well. But the intention of Peter and Mark in compiling their gospel was simply to provide a brief, fast-moving account of the life of Jesus. John, by contrast, takes much of that account for granted but seeks to make the personalities come alive. All the gospel writers mention the miracle of the feeding of the 5,000, but only John mentions that the boy's loaves were *barley* loaves. In the story of the calming of the sea only John mentions that the disciples had rowed between three and four miles from the shoreline. In recounting the crucifixion, only John observes that four soldiers were gambling for the seamless robe of his master.

Written in fifty years. The New Testament books were, in the main, written between AD50 and AD100.

Clearly Mark was written prior to the death of Peter. Since this occurred between AD64 and AD66 most authorities have assumed that Mark's gospel was set down at some time between AD55 and AD64.

Matthew's gospel is more difficult to date; the mention of practices connected with the temple and of the temple tax means that the book was certainly written before AD70, when the temple was destroyed. R. T. France favours AD63.[10]

However, Luke, who in addition to his gospel wrote the book of Acts and addressed both books to Theophilus, gives us a number of clues to work on. In some passages in the book of Acts he is writing in the third person; in others he is writing in the first person, making it clear that *he* was actually present. Luke wrote his gospel *before* he wrote the book of Acts. The book of Acts breaks off suddenly, for no logical reason. The simplest explanation for this is that Luke had no more to tell; his narrative had reached the present. Since 'the present' was the beginning of Paul's first imprisonment in Rome (*circa* AD61-AD63), Acts was obviously written before AD63 – and Luke's gospel even earlier.

John's writing almost certainly took place entirely in the 90s. However, J. A. T. Robinson believed that *all* the gospels, including John's, were written before AD70.[11] Certainly John's three letters were written to combat heresies that were entering the church in the 90s. John's book of Revelation – in which we find him peering down the corridor of the future towards apocalypse – was written from his exile on the island of Patmos. On the say-so of Eusebius we have tended to assume that John's banishment to Patmos occurred during the imperial reign of Domitian, though recent scholarship favours an earlier period. Hence the book of Revelation may well have been written before John's three letters (and most would say, before John's gospel): AD95 or even earlier.

Paul's letters. Most of the New Testament is taken up with letters, and most of these letters were written by Paul. Paul, whose original name was Saul, began as a member of the Jewish establishment and a persecutor of the Christians. His conversion to Christianity was the most dramatic of all and occurred on the road to Damascus.

After his conversion Paul went on a number of 'missionary journeys'. In each of these a team of assistants accompanied him. Together they raised up churches and encountered fierce persecution. To the churches he had established, Paul wrote his letters – often from a considerable distance – specifically to address problems occurring in those churches.

The letter to the Romans was the exception. When he wrote it Paul had never been to Rome and was, therefore, addressing no specific problems. That is why the book of Romans is the nearest thing in the New Testament to a systematic exposition of Christian theology. Hence it has been regarded as the most important book in the New Testament and the 'purest Gospel'. Frederic Louis Godet (1812-1900) said: 'Romans is the cathedral of the Christian faith.' William Tyndale wrote: 'Romans is the light and way into the whole of Scripture.'

It has been said that every revival in the history of Christianity has resulted from a study of the book of Romans. Certainly, the Reformation, led by Martin Luther, came as a direct result of Luther's understanding of justification by faith in Romans. In writing to the Roman church from Corinth in AD58, Paul was setting out the very essence of his belief in order to foster a strong church which, he might have hoped, would help him achieve his stated aim of evangelising Spain.

Paul wrote personal letters, too. Among them were the letters to Timothy and Titus. His second letter to Timothy is likely to have been his last. It was in this letter that he asked for his warm coat, his books and his parchments before the onset of winter (2 Timothy 4:9, 13). It is believed that he was beheaded in AD67.

Hence, while Paul was the major contributor to the New Testament, the distinction of the last writer is likely to belong to John. John, the beloved disciple of Jesus, is believed to have been the only apostle to die a natural death. He was the last of those forty writers whose collective works written over a period of

1,600 years have come to be known by Christians as the Bible.

References:
[1] Joshua 1:8; 8:33-35; 23:6, NIV.
[2] 1 Kings 2:3.
[3] 2 Kings 14:6; 22:8-23:24.
[4] Exodus 17:14; 24:4; Numbers 33:2.
[5] Acts 7:22.
[6] Mark 12:26 quotes Exodus 3:6.
[7] Luke 24:44.
[8] John 5:46, 47.
[9] Matthew 19:7, 8 (Deuteronomy 24:1); Mark 12:19 (Deuteronomy 25:5); John 1:17; 7:19 (Deuteronomy 4:44); John 1:45; Acts 3:22 (Deuteronomy 18:15); Hebrews 10:28 (Deuteronomy 17:2-7).
[10] R. T. France, *Tyndale New Testament Commentaries: Matthew*, page 30.
[11] Quoted in A. T. Hanson, *The Prophetic Gospel*, page 7.

* See chapter 19 on the dating of Moses and the Exodus.

How the books of the Bible were brought together

We have looked at the people who wrote the sixty-six books of the Bible, where possible given the approximate date *when* each book was written and, therefore, been able to estimate the total period between the time when the first book was penned and the last book completed.

But how were all these books brought together to be designated 'holy' or 'special'?

We need to answer the question in two halves, because the Bible is divided into two 'testaments', Old and New.

Books that were different

To Christians the Bible is a holy book. In fact, as we have seen, it is really a library of books. How did the thirty-nine books of the Old Testament and the twenty-seven books of the New Testament come to be considered especially 'holy' or 'different'?

We have already established that the Bible was, to say the least, *unusual*. The first of the forty authors of the Bible books (Moses) was separated from the last (John) by hundreds of years. The Bible writers belonged to a great many different walks of life, and had every conceivable level of education from the highest to the lowest. There were many diverse personality types. We have seen that among them were, on the one hand, herdsmen, shepherds, soldiers and fishermen; and, on the other, kings, legislators, statesmen, courtiers, priests and physicians.

Inevitably their literary styles reflected their very great differences. Some were writing law; others, religious poetry; still others, history; some, lyrical prose; others, lyrical poetry; some were writing in parables and allegories; others, biographies or personal memoirs and diaries; and some were writing prophecy; and still others, quite simply, personal correspondence.

With all this tremendous diversity, how were the sixty-six books deemed to be sufficiently 'different' or 'holy' to be included in what is called the 'canon' of the Bible?

The first thing to understand is that no individual or committee of individuals compiled the Bible. The Bible *grew*. This principle applies to both the Old and New Testaments. The unifying principle which makes the Bible holy, different, a living whole, is this: Christ himself, the bringer of salvation. As we watch the process by which the books were written and came to be accepted as God-breathed, we receive a sense that the One who was the unifying principle, the bringer of salvation, the source of inspiration, was also at work.

Books of the Old Testament. A great teacher wrote: 'Few realise that the Church of Christ possesses a higher warrant for her canon of the Old Testament than she does for her canon of the New.'[1]

The point he was making was that Jesus quoted and attributed authority to all parts of the Old Testament and, to his disciples after his resurrection, said that everything that had happened to him was a fulfilment of Old Testament prophecy. And Messianic prophecy was scattered throughout the Old Testament. Of course, because it had yet to be written, he could not give similar weight to the authority of the New Testament!

In the course of a clean-up in the temple in Josiah's reign the 'Book of the Law' was discovered. The book was presented to the King, and he read it. It had, he realised, been lost owing to the indifference of his predecessors. In former times, it had been kept in the tabernacle, then the temple, and the priests frequently read from it. The king had had a second copy. The recovery of the Book of the Law was seen by the King and later chroniclers as an event of great significance. The King read passages aloud to the people. The portions that were read came from Leviticus

26 and Deuteronomy 28 and 29. From this it may be deduced that the 'Book of the Law' represented the first five books of the Bible or, at least, part of them. The rediscovery of the book was used as a springboard for the reformation of the kingdom.

During the seventy years of the Exile, the words of the prophets, then extant, came to be valued a great deal. The nation had ceased to exist; and with it its capital and its temple. But there was still the Book of the Law – and there were the books of the prophets.

The Jewish *Talmud* asserts that Ezra, who led the people at the end of the Exile, undertook the collecting and editing of the Law and the Prophets. It also suggests that 'a Great Synagogue' was convened and that over a period of years all the Law, the Prophets and the Writings came under discussion. In addition to any work carried out by Ezra, many scholars have suggested that over the decades members of the Great Synagogue undertook the work of editing.

The Old Testament books are usually divided into four sections: The Pentateuch (the books of Moses), the historical books (Joshua to Esther), the five books of poetry and ethics (Job to the Song of Solomon), and the books of the prophets (Isaiah to Malachi).

The work of forming what we call the Old Testament had, thanks to Ezra and the Great Synagogue, begun as early as 450BC. Most scholars now accept that by the time of Christ the Old Testament existed in the form we have outlined.

Following the fall of Jerusalem in AD70, there was considerable discussion about the canon of Scripture. A rabbi called Yochanan ben Zakkai obtained written permission from the Roman authorities to convene the Council of Jamnia in order to discuss the canon of Scripture. However, the debate at that council simply centred around four books that were considered to be 'marginal': Proverbs, Ecclesiastes, the Song of Solomon and Esther. When the pros and cons with regard to these four books had been discussed, it was decided to include them within the canon, along with the rest of what we know as the Old Testament books. In fact, they could have done little else; 'the books which they decided to acknowledge as canonical were already generally accepted, although questions had been raised about them. Those (books) which they refused to admit had never been included. They did not expel from the canon any book which had previously been admitted.'[2]

The Council of Jamnia did not invest the books of the Bible with authority by including them in some sacred list. They were included in that list – the *canon* – because they were already acknowledged as God-inspired, authoritative, and had been, in most cases, for a number of centuries.

A contemporary of Christ, Philo of Alexandria, accepted the Old Testament canon in the form in which it is accepted today. The same is true of first-century Josephus Flavius. The earliest list of Old Testament books extant was drawn up by Melito, Bishop of Sardis, about AD170, and is preserved by Eusebius in the fourth volume of his *Ecclesiastical History.*[3]

Books of the New Testament. There are three categories of New Testament books: the narrative books (the four gospels and the Acts), the letters, and the apocalyptic book of Revelation which stands out on its own.

Although it took only fifty years to write the New Testament, it took far longer for it to assume the form that it has today. Not until AD367 do we find the New Testament books listed in exactly their present form. The list is contained in an Easter letter written by a Christian bishop, Athanasius.

In the two-and-a-half centuries or so between the completion of the last book of the New Testament and the list of Athanasius, there had been much discussion as to which books should or should not be included in the canon. The Old Testament formed the Scriptures of the earliest Christians; gradually some Christian writings were placed on a par with it, 'not by any decree of a council . . . but by the common agreement of the faithful; the spiritual intuition of the Church came slowly to decide which of its writings should be regarded as "canonical".'[4]

What brought about 'the common agreement of the faithful'? What informed 'the spiritual intuition of the Church'?

The books discarded from the Old Testament canon came to

be called the *Apocrypha*. A further group of wrongly attributed books – called the *Pseudepigrapha* – were also discarded. The Apocrypha contained history and wise sayings. The Pseudepigrapha contained a lot of magic and a little history. As we examine the books discarded from the New Testament canon – the New Testament 'Apocrypha' – again we sense the presence of supernatural guidance.

The books included were those accepted as God-inspired and proven in their ability to help men and to make Christ known. They were acknowledged to have been written by men close to Jesus and involved in the great first-century adventure which took the Christian Gospel to the limits of the then-known world.

A Greek contemporary of Athanasius spoke of 'the echo of a great soul' and professed to hear this echo in the canonical New Testament books. William Barclay has written: 'The ring of sublimity is to be found in the New Testament books. They carry their greatness on their faces. *They are self-evidencing.*'

When Bible translator J. B. Phillips came to compare the New Testament books 'with the writings which were excluded from the New Testament by the early "Fathers" ', he could only 'admire their wisdom'. He continued, 'Probably most people have not had the opportunity to read the apocryphal "gospels" and "epistles", although every scholar has. I can only say here that in such writings we live in a world of magic and make-believe, of myth and fancy. In the whole task of translating the New Testament I never for one moment, however provoked and challenged I might be, felt that I was being swept away into a world of spookiness, witchcraft and magical powers such as abound in the books rejected from the New Testament. It was the sustained down-to-earth faith of the New Testament writers which conveyed to me that inexpressible sense of the genuine and the authentic.' [5]

The 'self-evidencing' point comes across most powerfully when one reads the books that almost got into the New Testament but did not; books that were intended by their authors to be accepted, but were not.

In the second century a number of books were written called 'infancy gospels'. The four gospels of the canon provide little detail on the first three decades of the life of Jesus prior to the commencement of his public ministry. These infancy gospels were intended to 'fill in the gaps'.

The so-called 'gospel of Thomas' is supposed to give a record of the infancy of Jesus.

The child Jesus, while at play, is represented as creating live sparrows out of clay, and of striking dead a small child who 'ran and crashed against his shoulder'. Jesus the apprenticed carpenter is depicted stretching wooden beams like elastic and exercising an assortment of magical powers to no practical purpose.

No one could possibly mistake this for Scripture; nor has he. Scripture is *self-evidencing*. When you compare the gospels with these books, there is no question as to why some are 'in' and others, without argument, 'out'. The line is clear-cut. There is no room for debate.

Immense care was taken to ensure that the people who had authored the books that were accepted into the canon had known Jesus personally. The hallmark of these men was that they were concerned to demonstrate that the Jesus who *did* things in the past, is the living Christ who still does things.

In the book of Acts every single sermon finishes with the fact of the resurrection. For the New testament, Jesus was, above all, the living Christ. Because the four gospel writers were speaking about the living Christ, they gave a vastly disproportionate amount of space to the last week prior to his crucifixion and resurrection. The central concern of the disciples, of Christianity, of Christian theology, is the death and resurrection of Jesus. The books where this was not the central concern were quite simply either not considered or deliberately excluded from the canon.

'We may well believe,' says Professor F. F. Bruce, 'that those early Christians acted by a wisdom higher than their own in this matter, not only in what they accepted, but in what they rejected.' 'What is particularly important to notice is that the New Testament canon was not demarcated by the arbitrary decree of any Church Council. When at last the Church Council – the Synod of Hippo in AD393 – listed the twenty-seven books of the New Testament, it did not confer upon them any authority which they did not already possess, but simply recorded their previously established canonicity.'[6]

In short, the process by which the Books of the New Testament came to be accepted was, in all essential respects, the same process by which the Books of the Old Testament came to be accepted. Thus these two books — the Bible of the apostles and the Bible the apostles *wrote* — together came to comprise what Christians accept as the written Word of God.

References:

[1] G. A. Smith, *Modern Criticism and the Preaching of the Old Testament*, page 5.

[2] F. F. Bruce, *The Books and the Parchments*, page 89.

[3] Ibid, pages 89-92.

[4] G. W. H. Lampe (ed), *The Cambridge History of the Bible*, volume 2, page 42.

[5] J. B. Phillips, *Ring of Truth: A Translator's Testimony*, page 95.

[6] F. F. Bruce, *op cit*, pages 103, 104.

Note. For further information on the nature of biblical inspiration see the author's 'What did God have to do with it?', section 3 in *Experiencing the Power of the Word* (Autumn House).

2

Battle for the Bible

Moses lifted up the snake in the desert, so the Son of Man must be lifted up, 15that everyone who believes in him may have eternal life.d

16"For God so loved the world that he gave his one and only Son,e that whoever believes in him shall not perish but have eternal life. 17For God did not send his

a6 Or but spirit   b7 The Greek is plural.   c13 S
believes may have eternal life in him   e16 Or his
s21 Some interpreters end the quotation after ver

Surviving the centuries

We have seen how the Bible came to be written and approximately when. We have looked at the men who wrote it and glimpsed the reasons why it was written. We have traced the process by which the sixty-six books came to be accepted as the Holy Bible.

But the last book of the Bible was completed by the end of the first century AD.

Question: How did the sixty-six books survive the centuries, *especially* the centuries before Johann Gutenberg of Mainz invented printing in the 1430s?

Answer: It was laboriously copied out by hand thousands of times by generations of copyists.

Obvious conclusion: Since that process had been going on for well over a thousand years before the invention of printing, surely the whole text had to be riddled with mistakes and inaccuracies. And these mistakes and inaccuracies could only have been perpetuated when the Bible began to be printed.

Old Testament under fire

Controversy over the reliability and accuracy of the Bible came to a head in the eighteenth century, the Age of Reason. In particular it focused on the Old Testament. The Hebrew text of the Old Testament was based on manuscripts that were produced as late as the *ninth century AD*. They were the earliest manuscripts known.

Many scholars were adamant. The Bible could *not* be trusted. German scholar Friedrich Delitzsch spoke for scores of eighteenth, nineteenth and twentieth-century scholars when, in 1921, he wrote that the biblical text had experienced *'a degree of corruption beyond our wildest imagination'*.[1]

Until the 1940s such views represented the received wisdom. In 1939 British Museum curator and ancient manuscript authority Sir Frederic Kenyon wrote about the Masoretes who, for many centuries, had taken it upon themselves to copy out the Scriptures. The very oldest of their manuscripts dated from around AD900. It was, he said, most regrettable that generations of Jewish rabbis, for more than a thousand years, had viewed copies of holy Scripture with such superstitious veneration that as soon as they became old and worn the copies were reverently buried. Hence the absence of any Old Testament manuscripts to predate the Masoretic texts of the AD900s. By contrast, much earlier manuscripts of the New Testament survived and could be depended upon. The 'great and all-important question' was this: 'Does this Hebrew text [of the Old Testament], which we call Masoretic and which we have shown to descend from the texts drawn up about AD100, faithfully represent the Hebrew text as originally written by the authors of the Old Testament books?'[2]

Kenyon was charitable. At least he put it as a question. Most scholars presented an answer to the question similar to that of Friedrich Delitzsch: In the 1,300 years between the completion of Malachi and the oldest surviving Masoretic text, the Old Testament had been garbled beyond recognition.

Question: What *could* devout Jewish and Christian scholars do?

Answer: Come up with some inconclusive arguments before withdrawing in embarrassment. Among themselves they admitted: True enough; it was not reasonable to assume that, having used up the ink of thousands of copyists over ten centuries the Old Testament Scriptures had remained unchanged.

What was known of these copyists? Their habits, their reputation for accuracy?

The Masoretes

The Masoretes have a fascinating story.

When Roman General Titus left Jerusalem in smouldering ruins in AD70, he might have assumed that the mass slaughter that accompanied Jerusalem's fall – and the mass slaughter that had preceded it in the Galilean campaign – had crushed Judaism for ever.

When Roman General Silva, after the AD70-73 siege, entered the Zealot mountain stronghold of Masada to find that Eliezer and his supporters had committed mass suicide, *he* might have assumed that he had witnessed the last stand of Judaism.

When Roman Emperor Hadrian levelled Old Jerusalem in AD135 and built a Roman city *Aelia Capitolina*, over its base, he knew that scattered groups of hard-pressed Jews were to be found in Palestine and elsewhere; but was unlikely to have perceived them as in any way significant.

The Jewish religion had died with the destruction of the temple in AD70.

Or had it?

Judaism lived on without its temple and its system of sacrifices.

Judaism became a religion of sacred writings – and of scholars whose work was to preserve, copy and interpret them.

In AD110 Yohanan ben Zakkai chaired the Council of Jamnia. Rabbi Akiba ben Joseph (AD55-137) became its most prominent member. He had grown up as an illiterate orphan shepherd boy and his giant intellect had been stretched by ben Zakkai at the rabbinical school in Jamnia. Akiba sought to rally his scattered people around the sacred Scriptures. They were all that were left for the chosen people.

Akiba, based in Tverya (Tiberias), a city in Galilee, worked to standardise the Hebrew text. All subsequent copies and translations were based on Akiba's standardised text.

A group of scholars clustered around Akiba at Tiberias. A similar group of rabbis were working on similar projects in Babylonia. They worked both to translate and *interpret* the Scriptures.

Their chief concern was the *Torah* (or Law), the five books of

Moses. They sought to take the broad principles of the Law and apply them, in an infinity of ingenious ways, to all the complex situations of life. As a result the Tiberias scholars produced the *Mishnah*. The rabbis in Babylonia produced the *Gemara*. The two parts were joined together *circa* AD500 to become the *Talmud*.

Well before this time the groups of Jewish scholars in Tiberias and Babylonia had developed a high standard (tradition, *masorah*) of professionalism in order to preserve the purity of the biblical manuscripts they were copying. They devised a complicated system of safeguards against mistakes. Though always staying close to Akiba's standardised text, they *did*, from time to time, 'consider variant readings found in manuscripts at their disposal'.[3]

It was the widespread reverence for the Masoretic text of the Old Testament that led biblical scholars who lived centuries after the Masoretes had completed their work to be completely satisfied with its authenticity.

The Masoretes had been, after all, fanatics in their passion for accuracy and obsessive in their devotion to the tradition. The tradition to which they were devoted was that of passing down and recopying the sacred manuscripts across the centuries with the highest possible degree of accuracy.

The last Masoretic family was that of ben Asher of Tiberias. It is likely that they were responsible for the Masoretic *Codex of the Prophets* that survives in Leningrad.

'The all-important question'

The reputation of the Masoretes notwithstanding, the 'great, indeed all-important question' when Sir Frederic Kenyon completed the fourth edition of *Our Bible and the Ancient Manuscripts* in 1939 was: Could modern Bible scholars *really* believe that the Masoretes had preserved the thirty-nine books of the Old Testament free from error through eight centuries of copying?

Most answered, 'No'. It was alleged that much of what was taught about the Masoretes was myth. Far more likely – and a great deal more popular – was the establishment view typified by Friedrich Delitzsch that the biblical text had been corrupted 'beyond our wildest imagination'.

One day in 1947 that establishment view was unassailable.
The next day it came tumbling down.

What brought it down was a stone thrown by a young Bedouin in the vicinity of the Dead Sea.

References:

[1] Cited by Siegfried Horn, 'The Old Testament Text in Antiquity', *Ministry*, November 1987, pages 4-8.

[2] Sir Frederic Kenyon, *Our Bible and the Ancient Manuscripts*, fourth edition (1939), page 47.

[3] F. F. Bruce, *The Books and the Parchments*, revised edition (1984), page 107.

Dead Sea discoveries

When Muhammad ed Dhib, a young Bedouin shepherd, lobbed a stone into a hole in the wall of the mountain fronting the Dead Sea, he had no idea that the echo would be heard around the world. After all, he had only been out looking for a missing goat.

What he heard was the shattering of pottery. Wearily the lad pulled himself up the limestone cliffs, still calling the animal as he went.

Nearer to the opening then, he threw a second stone. Again the same sound; the breaking of pottery.

His curiosity heightened, the youth pulled himself up to the hole then peered into the gloom of a small cave. He had only an instant to look. His fingers lost their grip and he fell. But in that brief glimpse into the interior of the cave he had seen enough to fire his courage.

He climbed up a second time. He found a considerable number of cylindrical jars with distinctively shaped caps. Did they contain gold, jewels? Round about were the fragments of the jars his pebbles had broken.

His nose had scented something far more valuable than any goat. Belonging to the Ta'amireh tribe who wandered across the Wilderness of Judaea between Bethlehem and the Dead Sea, he ran with the speed and agility of one of the local ibexes to the shade of the hung animal skins, stakes and stench he called home.

He reported his find to an elder of his family. He, too, was interested and insisted on being taken to the spot.

The next day found them both cramped in the cave. They counted seven or eight jars. Some of them were empty. Others were filled with what looked like bundles of rags. They felt they might be on to something when they came across some folds of smooth brown leather.

With their finds they returned to the encampment. There irreverent hands unrolled a scroll almost 2,000 years old. It stretched from one end of the tent to the other. They were looking at what would become known as the larger of the two Isaiah scrolls.

It was felt that their find had been, after all, quite useless. They could not read the writing. The leather was too fragile to be put to any practical use. For a time, as the bedouins moved from place to place with their goats, they carried the scrolls with them and used them for trade with their neighbours. Some they kept, resolving to take them to Bethlehem. Perhaps there they would fetch a better price.

Market day in Bethlehem found them in earnest barter with a Syrian Christian, by trade a cobbler. He saw little practical value in the scrolls, but thought they might serve as raw materials for his shoe-mending business. Thereafter they were left littering the floor of his cobbler's shop for some days.

Then he had a bright idea. The characters on the ancient scrolls looked somehow intriguing. Up at Jerusalem there would be someone who could understand the writing and therefore the value of the scrolls. He took them to the Syrian convent of St Mark in the Old City. Only then did the cobbler realise that the scrolls had considerable monetary value.

Expeditions were organised to the caves. Soon every cave within the vicinity of the original find was being ransacked. Complete secrecy shrouded their operations; they were acting illegally. Under the laws of the British Mandate the authorities should have been informed immediately. Instead the Syrian Metropolitan began to hawk the fragments and the scrolls around the various scholarly institutions of Jerusalem to ascertain their exact worth. It was when they were shown to Professor E. L. Sukenik of the Hebrew University that the reverberations of the original find began to be felt around the world.

Dr John Trever, of the American School of Oriental Research, was the one who announced that what they were looking at was the scroll of Isaiah inscribed in Hebrew on papyrus from the pre-Christian period. 'You are holding,' he told the Metropolitan, 'the oldest manuscript of the Bible ever known.'

The story was out.

The original find had been made in March 1947. Then, almost twelve months later, archaeologists and specialists in ancient languages began to converge on the spot. The manuscripts discovered up to that time were moved to the Archaeological Museum (now known as the Rockefeller Museum), Jerusalem.

There was tremendous excitement in the scholarly world. The excitement soon communicated itself to the world of journalism, and a greater convergence of bodies massed in Jerusalem. Within a little more than twelve months of the original find, the 'Dead Sea Scrolls' were making headlines around the world.

Those questions which had been hammering on the door of Judaeo-Christian scholarship for so long were about to be answered.

The main finds were made in caves around Qumran. Soon the caves were numbered, Muhammad ed Dhib's cave being Cave I. Cave IV was a particularly rich one, containing 35,000 scroll fragments. Scholars, rather than Bedouins, took the lead in searching for more 'treasure'. Eventually ten manuscript-containing caves were found in the vicinity of Qumran, four in the Wadi Murabba'at near Bethlehem, a small number in a valley south of En-gedi, and a few more during excavations of Masada, where the Zealots had held out against General Silva from AD70 to 73.

The Essenes

During the period when the Seleucid Kings Antiocus III and Antiocus IV were enforcing the Greek language and culture on Palestine, a community of ultra-pious Jews established themselves at Qumran on the northern shores of the Dead Sea.

They were part of the reaction to the Hellenisation process.

While Jerusalem and Judaean Jews revolted under Maccabaean leadership, the Essenes were building a monastery (now excavated).

Behind their monastery was the limestone face of the Wilderness of Judaea, honeycombed with caves. Their lifestyle was ascetic and their leader known as the Teacher of Righteousness.

The earliest coins found on the Qumran site date from the reign of John Hyrcanus (134-104BC), and the latest coins date from the period AD132-135, the time of the second Jewish revolt. However, it would appear that the monastery was vacated in AD70 and that the period of occupation at the time of the second revolt was but a brief one. It is likely that the Essenes fled in AD70 when they learned of the approach of the Roman armies at the time of the fall of Jerusalem. Some unquestionably fled to Masada and perished with the Zealots there in AD73.

Central to the Qumran monastery had been the Scriptorium. Unquestionably an important part of the work of the Essene community was to copy out the Old Testament Scriptures, together with other literature. Among the manuscripts discovered in the caves was the *Manual of Discipline* or *The Rule of the Community*. This valuable document gives us an insight into the life and beliefs of the community. They lived, they believed, in an age of unparalleled wickedness. The days of judgement prophesied by Jeremiah and Ezekiel were at hand.

The aim of the Essenes was to study the Scriptures, interpreting them along the lines set down by their Teacher of Righteousness. The Messianic age was about to dawn. Until the dawn of that age they had to devote themselves to strict adherence to the law of God and to the study and reproduction of the sacred writings.

When they learned in AD70 of the mass slaughter in Galilee under Vespasian and later of the fall of Jerusalem at the hands of Titus, they might have thought that the new age had dawned. When they became aware that their own community was under attack, that might have given them reason for doubt. Their reaction must have been pre-planned, the caves pre-selected, the cylindrical vessels prepared. Whether the Roman slaughter represented an end or a beginning, of one thing the Essenes were determined: they would preserve for posterity the sacred Scriptures which they had – over time – so painstakingly set down.

The distribution of the cylindrical vessels containing the scrolls over such a wide area, in the most inaccessible of caves, was in itself a mammoth task. If it did, indeed, take place as the legions approached the monastery, it must have been undertaken with speed and great efficiency. Whatever their expectations or their fate, it is unlikely in the extreme that the Qumran Essenes expected that their sacred Scriptures would remain undiscovered for 1,877 years.

The Scrolls

Though some discoveries were still to be made, by the end of 1952 the scale of what had been found was apparent. Biblical scholars were beginning to refer to two eras in biblical studies: BQ and AQ, before Qumran and after Qumran.

In modern Jerusalem, not far from the Knesset, is a strangely shaped building. The visitor has to be informed that this modern building has been designed to resemble the shape of the curious caps from the cylindrically shaped vessels in which the scrolls had been found. It is called the Shrine of the Book. It has been built as a permanent home for the scrolls where the air is continually controlled and conditioned to facilitate their indefinite preservation. There the scrolls are on show, including one perfectly preserved scroll, the famous Isaiah scroll. Others are a little more fragmentary. But the fragments have, in many cases, been pieced together. The oldest manuscripts date from the third century BC. There is a wealth of non-biblical material. But the amount of biblical and biblically related material is overwhelming. Every Old Testament book is represented with the single exception of the book of Esther.

Significance of the discoveries

Until 1947 the most ancient Old Testament manuscript was the Masoretic text of AD900.

Suddenly everything had changed.

The central point of interest for those like W. F. Albright and Siegfried H. Horn, who converged on Jerusalem in the early 1950s, was to ascertain the extent to which the 2,000-year-old

Dead Sea Scrolls would uphold the accuracy of the Masoretic text and, therefore, the accuracy of the Old Testament accepted by Christians and Jews for so long.

Albright had been among the first to sense the importance of the scrolls. In the spring of 1948 he had told his students that the finds by the Dead Sea represented 'the greatest manuscript discovery of modern times'. In the months and years thereafter he, and many others, spent thousands of hours poring over detailed photographs of the scrolls.

The scrolls were categorised, identified and pieced together. Some scholars were particularly interested in what the non-biblical scrolls could teach them about the Essenes and the century in which they had lived. Others, like Albright, were concerned with the all-important comparison between the Hebrew content of the scrolls and the Hebrew Old Testament, based on the Masoretic text of AD900 (for two centuries dismissed by many experts as a corrupted copy of the Scriptures that were extant at the time of Christ).

More was at stake than the reputation of the Masoretes as copyists. The real issue was the dependability of an important part of the source upon which Christian doctrine was based, the Scriptures revered by Jews and Christians.

By 1952 the careful comparison of the contents of Cave I (dating from the time of Christ) with the Masoretic text (dating from the tenth century) was complete. *The texts were, to all practical purposes, identical.* Differences were almost exclusively composed of spelling mistakes, or of a grammatical nature. At no point did they affect the sense of the biblical text then in use. It appeared that the Hebrew Bible extant in the days of Jesus was the same as the Masoretic text from which the Old Testament of the twentieth century had been translated. The Isaiah scroll from Cave I, much abused by the Bedouins and the Bethlehem cobbler, contained a text form virtually identical with the printed Hebrew Bibles then in use.

As the years passed and the contents of the other caves were examined and compared, much was learned. There had been a few minor omissions and additions, but the Masoretic text reflected the scrolls fairly faithfully. In places the content of the scrolls was closer to the Septuagint (the Greek translation of the Old Testament) than the Masoretic text. This illustrated that the Septuagint translators had followed a Hebrew 'revised version' different from the revision favoured by the Masoretes. But, these minor considerations aside, the message of the Dead Sea Scrolls was this: *the text of the Old Testament had been preserved unchanged down the centuries.*

But what of the experts who, since the eighteenth century, had taught that down the centuries the biblical text had experienced 'a degree of corruption beyond our wildest imagination'? And what of the thousands who had believed them?

Most were dead. Others embarrassed. Many admitted that, after all, the Masoretic Bible was essentially the same as the Bible of Jesus and the apostles. A few, however, prepared to fight another day. . . .

Controversy over the Scrolls

As the closeness of the Dead Sea manuscripts with the Hebrew Bible was being demonstrated, the critics began to attack the genuineness of the scrolls themselves.

As each wave of criticism and counter-assertion emerged from Jerusalem and from the university campuses of the Western countries, the controversy was reported by the world's press. Rarely had the pronouncements of fusty academics made such headlines.

In Europe and the United States the dating of the scrolls – from the third century BC (very largely) to AD70 – was hotly contested.

But as more scientific explorations took place and more scientific tests were applied, the age and genuineness of the scrolls were upheld.

As the Qumran monastery was excavated, the evidence of pottery, coinage and other artefacts attested to the fact that the Essenes had occupied the site throughout the last three centuries before Christ and until AD70. There was then evidence of a brief Roman occupation of the site. Finally, scholars found artefacts which pointed to a further period of Jewish occupation at the time of the second Jewish revolt of AD135. Thus the archaeological evidence authenticated the dating of the manuscripts.

There was, in addition, scientific evidence. The linen wrappers containing the scrolls were subjected to carbon-14 dating tests. The great majority of the scrolls were dated to the three centuries before Christ, a few to the century after Christ, and a very few to the second century AD (coincident with the occupation of the site during the second Jewish revolt).

Again the critics were silent. It was agreed that the age and genuineness of the scrolls were beyond dispute.

Sources:

Hershel Shanks (ed), *Understanding the Dead Sea Scrolls* (SPCK).
Robert Eisenman and Michael Wise (eds), *The Dead Sea Scrolls Uncovered.*
Siegfried Horn, *The Spade Confirms the Book* (second edition).
J. A. Thompson, *The Bible and Archaeology* (third edition).
J. M. Allegro, *The Dead Sea Scrolls.*
John Allegro, *The Dead Sea Scrolls: A Reappraisal.*
Edmund Wilson, *The Dead Sea Scrolls: 1947-1969.*
W. H. Brownlee, *The Meaning of the Qumran Scrolls for the Bible.*

The Battle for the New Testament

The battle for the Old Testament was won with the aid of a discovery made by a Bedouin goatherd. The battle for the New Testament was won with the aid of a discovery by a German professor.

The Bedouin's discovery occurred by accident and was accomplished in seconds. The German's discovery occurred after years of search that served to occupy much of his career.

The German professor's name: Constantin Tischendorf.

A professor's mission

Trained in the theology school of the University of Leipzig, Tischendorf, with such a background, was not an obvious candidate to be a defender of the New Testament. In the year in which he took his doctorate – 1838 – the conventional wisdom among German scholars was hotly opposed to the reliability of the New Testament. But Tischendorf was prepared to stand out against it.

His studies led him to the view that the gospels were authored not only by eye witnesses of the events recorded but by Matthew, Mark, Luke and John specifically, and that the text was entirely to be trusted. While other German theologians asserted that Paul wrote only four of the letters attributed to him – Romans, 1 and 2 Corinthians and Galatians – Tischendorf's careful examination of language and style led him to the view that Paul had written them all.

Soon he found himself right at the centre of the nineteenth-century debate on whether the New Testament was reliable. Edward Gibbon in *The Decline and Fall of the Roman Empire* – written in the previous century – had launched the debate with his assertion that early Christian leaders 'with rash and sacrilegious hands' had tampered with the original New Testament manuscripts. Richard Porson of Cambridge made a crusade out of New Testament criticism.

Heinrich Paulus of Heidelberg and David Strauss of Zurich were soon attacking the whole miraculous content of the New Testament. Tischendorf's 'work came not a moment too soon'.[1]

It frustrated Tischendorf that biblical critics were able so easily to uncover inaccuracies in vernacular Bibles. He was angry that Bible translators, from Martin Luther down to translators of his own century, had used the Greek New Testament of Erasmus (1516) so uncritically. He believed that the work of the Dutch Renaissance scholar was slapdash and deeply flawed. What was needed, he decided, was an accurate text of the New Testament, based on the most ancient of manuscripts. He decided to spend his life discovering just such a manuscript. It would, he wrote, confound 'the dazzling wit and ingenious sophistry' of those who 'torture and twist the facts which occurred 1,800 years ago'. 'I am confronted by a sacred task,' wrote Tischendorf to his wife Angelika, 'the struggle to regain the original form of the New Testament.'

First attempt

There were four ancient manuscripts of the New Testament when Tischendorf began his search. The first, the *Codex Alexandrinus*, was 1,300 years old and owned by the British Museum. The second, the *Codex Claramontanus*, was almost as old and owned by the national library of Paris. Both manuscripts were incomplete.

The other two ancient manuscripts were the *Codex Vaticanus* and the *Codex Ephraemi*. The first, dated from the middle of the fourth century, was owned by the Vatican and not available to any Protestant scholar. The second was accessible in Paris but unreadable. Its fifth-century text of the Bible had been more or less erased a few centuries after it had been written, and the writings of Syrian scholar Ephraem inscribed over it.

The difficulties facing Tischendorf in finding a new, definitive edition of the Greek New Testament were formidable!

He accepted them as a challenge.

He would, he said, produce his definitive Greek New Testament within the year!

He went to Paris. There he abused his eyes by spending months poring over the faded *Codex Claramontanus* and the largely erased *Codex Ephraemi*. With super-human effort he managed to transcribe sixty-four faded Old Testament leaves and 145 largely erased New Testament pages.

At the British Museum, like many before him, he was given unrestricted access to the *Codex Alexandrinus*.

It was in Rome that he was stone-walled. After initially being refused access to the *Codex Vaticanus*, he persisted with his pressure. At last he was permitted just six hours with it.

As promised, his Greek New Testament was ready within the year. But he was dissatisfied. In his heart he knew that it was little better than that produced by Berlin professor Karl Lachmann in 1831. Even the best of the manuscripts to which he had limited access contained only parts of the New Testament.

He decided: as yet undiscovered manuscripts had to be found on which to establish the authentic text of the New Testament.

Rumours from the East

In 1838 American archaeologist Dr Edward Robinson made one of his celebrated trips to the Middle East. At the same time Tischendorf was committing to paper the belief that 'in some recess of the Greek or Coptic, Syrian or Armenian monasteries, there might be some precious manuscript slumbering for ages in dust and darkness'. Edward Robinson confirmed his hunch. He reported that in St Catherine's monastery on Mount Sinai there was a large and untouched library of the most ancient manuscripts imaginable.

Tischendorf was not to know it, but St Catherine's – for reasons embedded in its unique history and unbeknown to anyone – contained the largest collection of the most ancient biblical manuscripts in the world. And among them was 'a jewel beyond price'.

St Catherine's is the oldest continuously inhabited monastery in Christendom. It was founded by order of the Emperor Justinian in AD527 and named in honour of Catherine, a Christian martyr spiked and beheaded in AD307.

A vast number of monasteries were founded during the Byzantine period. In their early years, like St Catherine's, they would have sought to accumulate libraries of manuscripts. However, most if not all fell prey to one or other of the waves of invaders who periodically swept across the Middle East.

What preserved the library of St Catherine's from the sackings in which many of the other monastic libraries perished was the political tradition there. That tradition was the settled policy not only of political non-alignment but of actively currying favour with each successive conqueror. By the nineteenth century all the monks of St Catherine's were Greek. In earlier centuries there had been a mix of Greeks, Syrians, Georgians and Ethiopians. The multi-national nature of the group had helped perpetuate the political flexibility which preserved their library, and them, from destruction.

In AD625 the monks sent a delegation to Muhammad himself, begging his protection. This was to be the beginning of their uniquely tolerant relationship with Islam. Annually they petitioned Constantinople, requesting continued protection. In AD1115 they petitioned Crusader King Baldwin of Jerusalem *not* to pay them a visit! They wanted above all to avoid alienating the Sultan.

Tischendorf and the Christian world were to have reason to be grateful to the monks whose careful diplomacy had preserved the manuscripts through many centuries of blood-letting and destruction.

On the track

Mount Sinai is a triangle of mountains, a rock barrier between Asia and Africa. From the summit, 2,260 metres above sea level, the view is one of gaunt ridges and cragged peaks exuding the breath of the Old Testament. This moonscape is bluish in the shade, lion-coloured where the sun penetrates, sometimes rippled and sometimes scooped out into whorls.

This is the setting for the monastery of St Catherine.

In March 1844 Tischendorf took ship from Italy for Alexandria. From Alexandria he made his way to Cairo. Monks representing St Catherine's were there to meet him. They told him they had priceless manuscripts at the monastery, but something in their tone told Tischendorf that they had no idea *how* priceless.

The journey from Cairo to Mount Sinai was a hazardous one. It took twelve days to reach the Plain of Raha from which rises the northern extremity of Mount Sinai.

At the monastery a basket was let down. Tischendorf placed in it a letter of recommendation he had brought with him. The basket was drawn up into the monastery. When it was let down again the monks had attached a crossbar to it. Tischendorf first, then the remainder of his party, were drawn up one by one.

The monastery's literary treasures were contained in the narthex. To reach the huge wooden doors of the narthex, Tischendorf had to descend steeply. The church was lower than almost any other part of the interior of the monastery walls, and the narthex was like an ante-nave.

The narthex or library was, according to Tischendorf, 'a poor place to which no one in the monastery paid much attention'. Nevertheless, the appointed librarian Kyrillos was helpful. As Tischendorf perused the manuscripts one by one in the course of May 1844, Kyrillos extended to him a courtesy that few more professional librarians would have permitted. Tischendorf was allowed to take the priceless manuscripts from the narthex and examine them at his leisure in his own room.

Towards the end of May he felt he had found 'the pearl of all my researches'. 'I perceived in the middle of the great hall a large and wide basket full of old parchments; and the librarian, who was a man of information, told me that two heaps of papers like these, mouldered by time, had been already committed to the flames. What was my surprise to find amid this heap of papers a considerable number of sheets of a copy of the Old Testament in

Greek, which seemed to me to be one of the most ancient that I had ever seen.'

Of the 129 parchments Tischendorf examined, Kyrillos permitted him to take forty-three home with him. With these parchments he returned to Cairo.

In 1846 Tischendorf published a brilliant edition of the forty-three parchments under the title *Codex Frederico-Augustanus*. The King of Saxony had paid his expenses; it seemed right to him that his findings should bear the king's name.

The discovery

But Tischendorf had not found that for which he was searching: an ancient and complete manuscript of the New Testament. In 1853 he set off again, visiting monasteries in Lilya, Cairo, Alexandria, Jerusalem, Laodicea, Smyrna and Constantinople, as well as St Catherine's in Sinai.

At St Catherine's he asked the monks to produce the eighty-seven parchments he had seen nine years earlier. For reasons best known to themselves they refused to allow him access and, indeed, denied all knowledge of the existence of the parchments. Nevertheless Tischendorf returned with the finds from the other monasteries and was able to publish, based on them, an improved edition of the Greek New Testament.

As the months went by, the dusty depths of St Catherine's occupied Tischendorf's imagination. He felt that there were many treasures there still to be uncovered and that the monks were perhaps deliberately preventing him from having access to them.

Soon a third visit to St Catherine's was being planned. This time the finance came from the Tsar of Russia. The condition imposed by the Tsar was that any discoveries made by Tischendorf were to become the Tsar's property.

The third visit, at first, promised to be even more disappointing than the second. After several days of foraging among the dust clouds in the narthex of St Catherine's, Tischendorf grew impatient. He told his companions that he would give it another three days and then return to Cairo.

This three-day period proved to be vital. In it he uncovered 346 parchments (all in the same handwriting) – including a codex which contained the whole of both the Old and the New Testaments. It was of incredible age.

Tischendorf had uncovered the pearl of great price; achieved the aim of a lifetime.

To his wife he wrote: 'It is the only such manuscript in the world. Neither the *Codex Vaticanus* nor the London *Alexandrinus* contains the whole New Testament, and the *Sinai Codex* is undoubtedly older than both. This discovery is a remarkable occurrence and a great one for Christian knowledge.' Tischendorf was not exaggerating.

References:
[1] James Bentley, *Secrets of Mount Sinai*, page 29.

The find of a lifetime

Tischendorf made his great discovery in the monastery on Mount Sinai in 1859.

The *Codex Sinaiticus* – the complete Old and New Testaments in 'book' as opposed to 'scroll' form – was older than the oldest manuscript extant. Tischendorf was sure that it dated from very early in the Christian era. 'I was', he wrote, 'beside myself with joy.'

It is regrettable for his reputation that Tischendorf, at this point, allowed his enthusiasm to get the better of him.

The Russian connection

Remembering his promise to the Tsar – a condition agreed to in haste to secure finance for his third venture – Tischendorf began to make plans to remove the Codex from its home on Sinai. In addition to his promise it is likely that his reasoning went something like this: Only by removing this priceless manuscript from the place where it has been ignored for so long can the world be given an extraordinary enrichment of Christian knowledge.

With others, Tischendorf accomplished the time-consuming task of copying out the Codex. At the same time he sought to implant in the minds of the monks the idea of making a presentation of the Codex to the Tsar.

But the minds of the monks had been much altered since his first visit in 1842. They were loath to allow any manuscript out of the monastery. The best Tischendorf could do was to persuade them to make the Codex not a gift but a loan to the Tsar.

With this ruse he wrested the Codex from its home and removed it to St Petersburg. The monks were never to see their Codex again.

'On 19 November 1859,' wrote Tischendorf, 'I presented to their Imperial Majesties, in the Winter Palace, . . . my rich collection of Greek, Syriac, Coptic, Arabic and other manuscripts in the middle of which the Sinaiticus Bible shone like a crown.' There was not so much as a whisper that the Sinaiticus Bible was not his to give.

Soon Tischendorf was under pressure from the Tsar and the leaders of the Russian Orthodox Church to publish the *Codex Sinaiticus*. This was a task of immense complexity. Like other very early manuscripts – including the originals on which the actual authors of Scripture would have set down their narratives – the *Codex Sinaiticus* contained no divisions into paragraphs, no spaces between the words and no punctuation. Needless to say, it contained no division into verses or chapters.

Tischendorf tackled his task with a will. In 1862, 223 copies were presented by the Tsar to the great libraries of the world. With no sense of irony whatever, the Tsar presented one copy to the monastery on Mount Sinai. There it remains on display in place of the original. Eventually the monks agreed to sign over their precious manuscript to the Tsar in exchange for a gift of 9,000 roubles and certain political concessions.

How the Codex came to Britain

The *Codex Sinaiticus* remained at St Petersburg – renamed Petrograd, then Leningrad – through the Bolshevik Revolution. Financial pressures following the revolution led the leaders of the Soviet Union to offer priceless manuscripts for sale. In 1933 information reached Sir Frederic Kenyon of the British Museum that the Soviet government was planning to sell the *Codex Sinaiticus* for £200,000. He immediately began to canvass support for the project but, in the event, was able to offer only £40,000. The Soviets then reduced their price to £100,000. Sir Frederic felt that that was not an opportunity to be missed. He arranged a consultation with Prime Minister Ramsay McDonald and the Archbishop of Canterbury. Both were soon as excited about the project as Sir Frederic himself. Sir Frederic was given authority to raise his bid to £60,000. But the Russians stuck out for their £100,000.

Immediately prior to Christmas 1933, at the height of the Depression, the National Government put the project of the *Codex Sinaiticus* before the nation. They would guarantee to pay half the price if the British public would come up with the other half.

Collections were made from door to door. Despite the public's massive unemployment and immense privation the required sum of money was raised.

The *Codex Sinaiticus* arrived at the British Museum in a taxi — with a *Daily Express* reporter for company.

The significance of the Codex

Tischendorf died, aged 59, in the belief that he had achieved his life's objective. He had provided the world with a witness to the pure, uncorrupted text of the Scriptures; above all, of the New Testament.

In the same year in which the Codex itself was published — 1862 — Tischendorf published a book expounding the significance of it. With the *Codex Vaticanus*, he maintained (correctly), the *Codex Sinaiticus* was one of the two earliest copies of the whole Greek Bible. Though there was some argument as to the date of the Sinai Bible, all the experts were prepared to accept Tischendorf's view that it was written in the early-to-mid fourth century (*circa* AD300-350).

Since Tischendorf's death the pieces of the jigsaw have been placed together. In AD331 the Emperor Constantine ordered Eusebius of Caesarea to superintend the copying of fifty accurate manuscripts of the Bible. Constantine even specified the type of parchment on which they were to be written. Eusebius was to secure the service of the most professional scribes available.

Eusebius apparently superintended the task, and the fifty copies were produced to the highest possible standard.

It is widely believed that both the *Codex Sinaiticus* and the *Codex Vaticanus* were among those fifty copies.

No one knows for certain how the *Codex Sinaiticus* came into the possession of St Catherine's monastery. It was written centuries before St Catherine's was founded. It is, however, known that it was once treasured in the library of Caesarea. Tischendorf's first visit to St Catherine's had yielded forty-three manuscripts; among them had been the notes of a scribe. From those notes he had learned that almost all of the manuscripts had originated in Caesarea.

Since Caesarea was taken by the Arabs in AD638, it can reasonably be conjectured that the *Codex Sinaiticus* – among many other manuscripts – was saved and taken by refugees from Caesarea to the remote monastery on Mount Sinai.

Since Tischendorf's discovery of the *Codex Sinaiticus* and the publication of his commentary no serious revision of the Bible has been undertaken with recourse to them.

The English Authorised Version (the King James Bible) was published in 1611 and based on translation work undertaken earlier by, among others, William Tyndale. The manuscripts from which the translators had worked had been of much later date than the *Codex Sinaiticus*. Hence it was the concern of many scholars in the late nineteenth century to examine the King James Bible critically with the *Codex Sinaiticus* for reference. Among those scholars were B. F. Westcott and F. J. A. Hort.

What they found was not earth-shattering, but interesting nevertheless. Those who, through the centuries, copied out by hand the books of the New Testament were, it would appear, guilty of a number of minor errors. In English translations of the New Testament undertaken since that time, the variations between the texts have been indicated by footnotes, for example, 'not found in older manuscripts'.

The following represents a sample of the major variations:

The second half of Matthew 6:13 (KJV) reads: *'For thine is the kingdom, and the power, and the glory, for ever. Amen.'* This is absent from both the *Codex Vaticanus* and the *Codex Sinaiticus*.

John 8:1-11 (KJV) is the story of the woman taken in adultery. The story is absent from both the *Codex Vaticanus* and the *Codex Sinaiticus*.

Mark 9:43 (second half) and 44 present a picture of hell, beloved by hell-fire preachers of bygone centuries; *'the fire that shall never be quenched: where their worm dieth not, and the fire is not quenched'*. This is absent from the *Codex Sinaiticus*.

John 4:9 (last part): *'For the Jews have no dealings with the Samaritans.'* That helpful historical comment is not found in the *Codex Sinaiticus*.

John 5:4 (KJV) reads: *'For an angel went down at a certain season into the pool, and troubled the water: whosoever then first after the troubling of the water stepped in was made whole of whatsoever disease he had.'* That rather strange addition to the story of the man at the Pool of Bethesda is absent from the *Codex Sinaiticus*.[1]

Like Tischendorf, Westcott and Hort believed that those minor additions/alterations had either happened accidentally or had occurred when a fragment of commentary from the margin had been incorporated into the text. They believed that occasionally the scribes had misread/misheard words; more rarely, had mistranslated them.

In their Introduction to *The New Testament and the Original Greek*, Westcott and Hort wrote: 'It will not be out of place to add here a distinct expression of our belief that even among the numerous unquestionably spurious readings of the New Testament there are no signs of deliberate falsification of the text for dogmatic purposes. . . . Often the additions to the text which are found in the later documents but not in the Sinaiticus are merely harmless, and indeed sometimes positively useful additions.'

Edward Gibbon and other eighteenth- and early nineteenth-century scholars had believed that early Christian leaders had 'with sacrilegious hands' made major alterations in the New Testament text. The discoveries of Tischendorf and the careful scholarship of others have uncovered only minor, trivial differences. None, certainly, that has the slightest bearing on Christian belief. Thanks to the *Codex Sinaiticus* we can say with assurance that in the New Testament of our twenty-first-century Bibles we have to all intents and purposes the gospels, books and letters as written down by their first-century authors.

After discussing the slight variations between the New Testament portion of the *Codex Sinaiticus* and the later manuscripts on which the contemporary Bible was based, Sir Frederic Kenyon, in 1939, stated: 'Our Bible, as we have it today, represents as closely as may be the actual words used by the authors of the sacred books.'[2]

References:
[1] Sir Frederic Kenyon, *Our Bible and the Ancient Manuscripts*, gives a detailed account of the textual variations. See pages 16 *et seq*; Appendix 1, pages 247-256.
[2] Ibid, page 18.

Sources:
James Bentley, *Secrets of Mount Sinai*.
S. L. Greenslade (ed.), *The Cambridge History of the Bible: from the Reformation to the Present Day*, volume 3.
Benson, Bobrick, *The Making of the English Bible*.
David Daniell, *William Tyndale: a Biography*.
Brian Moynahan, *If God Spare My Life: William Tyndale, The English Bible and Sir Thomas More*.
John Drane, *Introducing the New Testament*.
John Drane, *Jesus and the Four Gospels: An Illustrated Documentary*.
Siegfried Horn, *Records of the Past Illuminate the Bible*.
Sir Frederic Kenyon, *The Bible and Modern Scholarship*.
Sir Frederic Kenyon, *The Story of the Bible*.
Sir Frederic Kenyon, *Our Bible and the Ancient Manuscripts*.
B. F. Westcott, *A General View of the History of the Ancient Bible* (third edition).

The battle won

The battle for the New Testament had been at its fiercest in the mid-nineteenth century.

F. C. Baur of the 'Tubingen School' had declared nearly all the books of the New Testament to be unauthentic. By 'unauthentic' Baur and his followers meant that the New Testament books could not have been written by either the dates or the authors assigned to them. The only exceptions they were prepared to make were for Paul's letters to the Romans, the Corinthians and the Galatians.

But the Dutch school of van Manen went even further. Their message was: *None* of the New Testament books was written in the first century or by anyone who had firsthand knowledge of the life of Jesus.

In England the climax of the sceptical movement was in the work of W. R. Cassels. His book *Supernatural Religion* (1871-77) was a thoroughgoing attack on belief in miracles and on the date, authority and authenticity of the books of the New Testament.[1]

Clearly the discoveries of Constantin Tischendorf represented a grievous blow to the German, Dutch and English schools of criticism. By discovering a handwritten Greek version of the Bible at the Sinai monastery, by uncovering historical evidence which dated it between AD300 and AD350, and by linking it with the *Codex Vaticanus* ('under wraps' at the Vatican for many centuries but then proved to be of approximately the same age as the *Codex Sinaiticus*), Tischendorf had put the critics on the defensive. But he had not put them to rout.

'The merest fragment'

The critics lived to fight another day.

There remained, they argued, a significant period between the first-century dates assigned to the New Testament books and the period out of which the *Codex Sinaiticus* and the *Codex Vaticanus* had emerged. Conservative Christian scholars were challenged to provide 'the merest fragment' of a manuscript from between the first century, when the New Testament books were assumed to have been written, and the fourth century in the early part of which Sinaiticus and Vaticanus had been written.

That was an enormous challenge!

The critics had reason to believe that the challenge could never be met. And conservative biblical scholars feared that the critics were right.

Sinaiticus and *Vaticanus* dated from the period when the principal material for book production was *vellum*. Vellum was durable and, as had been demonstrated, could survive for many centuries. But the critics and the conservative biblical scholars knew full well that before the early fourth century the book material in general use in the Graeco-Roman world was *papyrus*. And they knew, equally well, that papyrus was noted for its perishability.

Even the most optimistic of Christian scholars felt that 'the gap' between AD100 and AD300 would never be bridged.

But they were wrong.

More treasures on Sinai

In 1891 papyrus documents began to flow from the warm sands of Egypt to the libraries and museums of Europe and the United States of America.[2]

St Catherine's had yet more treasures to yield. The monks in their isolated fastness on Sinai had been, to say the least, rather suspicious of the outside world since Tischendorf had removed from them their precious Codex. It took the studied tact and charm of two highly accomplished Orientalists from Cambridge, Mrs Lewis and Mrs Gibson (twin sisters) to thaw out their icy reserve. After many months of research and study, the two Orientalists discovered a partially erased copy of the gospels in Syriac. This copy predated all earlier discoveries up to that time and was generally agreed to have been made before AD200.

Before anyone had had time to analyse the tremendous significance of what the two ladies had discovered on Sinai, Dr Ezra Abbot called attention to a commentary on the four gospels in Armenian which he had been studying for a decade or more. This commentary, called in Greek *Diatessaron*, dated from a period earlier than AD170. But its significance did not stop with its early date. It indicated that by AD170 the gospels of Matthew, Mark, Luke and John were 'held in undisputed pre-eminence over all other narratives' of the life of Christ. In short: as early as AD170 the gospels had acquired a sanctity that only great age could have given them.[3]

By then the massed battalions of the critics were falling back on many fronts.

The warm sands of Egypt

The papyrus documents discovered in the warm, preserving sands of Egypt at the turn of the century related to both testaments. There were portions of the book of Genesis and of the Psalms which dated from the fourth century. There was a collection of the sayings of Jesus — most of which were to be found in the gospels — which dated from the third century. There was a considerable portion of the letter to the Hebrews that dated from the third century.[4]

At Dura, on the banks of the Euphrates, in 1920 a group of British army officers made an accidental discovery. The archaeologists were brought in. They identified what had been found as a Roman fort and, in the succeeding years, made a complete excavation of it. Evidence was found which enabled them to piece together its history. It had, for example, been taken by the Persians in AD256. Prior to its fall its walls had been strengthened by the material left after the destruction of a quantity of houses, a synagogue and a Christian church. Among the debris was found a number of papyri and vellum manuscripts which had been pro-

tected from the damp in a manner similar to that which had survived the centuries in the Egyptian sands. Among these was a
fragment of the already discovered *Diatessaron* – the commentary on the four gospels in Greek – 'written in a hand of the first
half of the third century'.[5] As with Dr Abbot's *Diatessaron*, the
scholars were provided with a mosaic of passages from all four
gospels. Scholars agreed that this proved that the *Diatessaron*
had existed in Greek before AD150, and that this 'Commentary'
on the gospels was likely to have been in circulation well before
the date when the sceptics believed that the gospels themselves
had been written![6]

Bridging the 'gap'

The earliest generation of German, Dutch and English critics
was long-since dead. The discomfiture of those who had accepted, taught and popularised their viewpoints increased with every
new discovery.

But the worst, for them, was yet to come. The conservative
Bible students were to have their greatest triumph since the discovery of the *Codex Sinaiticus*. The new discovery has generally
been referred to as the *Chester-Beatty Biblical Papyri*.

The discovery was made in 1930. The exact story surrounding
the find is known only to the locals who made it. The find was
made in a Coptic graveyard near the Nile. Like the Dead Sea
Scrolls (at that point undiscovered in their caves) these papyri
were enclosed in a number of earthenware jars. The bulk of the
find was acquired by Mr A. Chester-Beatty, an American collector
who lived in England. A small number of fragments were pur-
chased by the University of Michigan. The discovery was first
reported in *The Times* on 17 November 1931. The report
announced that a large library of biblical papyri had been discovered and that it consisted of portions of twelve manuscripts of
which eight contained books of the Old Testament, and three
manuscripts contained books of the New Testament. All agreed
with British Museum curator Sir Frederic Kenyon that the papyri
were 'older by a century or more than the oldest manuscripts
(other than very small fragments) hitherto known'.

The Chester-Beatty collection included two substantial manuscripts of Genesis, one from the third, the other from the early fourth century. Between them they covered the greater part of the book. There were manuscripts of Numbers and Deuteronomy – dating from the first half of the second century! (That is, between AD100 and AD150.) There was a fragmentary manuscript of Isaiah which dated from the third century, a portion of Jeremiah dating from the late second or early third century, and manuscripts of Ezekiel, Daniel and Esther from the same period.

The papyri covering the New Testament books aroused the most interest. One of them had started life as a copy of all four gospels, plus the book of Acts. It had been written in a small hand which scientists trained in deciphering ancient manuscripts agreed in assigning to the first half of the third century. In other words, a full century earlier than either *Sinaiticus* or *Vaticanus*. Portions of thirty leaves have been preserved out of the original total of 110. Two contained portions of Matthew's gospel, six of Mark's gospel, seven of Luke's gospel, two of John's gospel, and thirteen of the book of Acts. Sections of Paul's letters to the Romans, Philippians, Colossians and of his first letter to the Thessalonians were found at an earlier stage. Later it was discovered that all of Paul's letters were present in excellent condition. Foremost of papyrologists, Professor V. Wilcken, dated them to about the year AD200.[7]

The third New Testament manuscript in the Chester-Beatty collection contained a part – approximately one third – of the book of Revelation. That was dated to the third century.

Light on the resurrection puzzle

Meanwhile the significance of an earlier discovery began to be appreciated. Charles Freer of Detroit, travelling in Egypt, found portions of a vellum manuscript which he recognised as being biblical in content. The manuscripts were in the possession of a Cairo dealer. Freer bought them for the United States. They included one of the earliest copies of the gospels in Greek. In addition there were two Old Testament manuscripts covering Deuteronomy and Joshua, dating from the fifth or possibly early sixth century, plus fragments of the earlier books of Moses, together with the book of Ruth. There was a damaged copy of the Psalms dating from the sixth century. There was another New Testament manuscript including the gospels and the epistles dating from the fourth or fifth century. Collectively, Freer's finds became known as the *Washington Codex*.

The *Washington Codex* was of interest for more reasons than one. It not only represented another major find in terms of ancient biblical manuscripts; it also helped scholars to understand something that had concerned them since the discovery of the *Codex Sinaiticus*. One of the omissions from the *Codex Sinaiticus* had been the last twelve verses of the gospel of Mark. While containing the Resurrection accounts in detail from the other three gospels, the *Codex Sinaiticus* ends the gospel of Mark with the announcement of the Resurrection, but omits subsequent details, including the commission addressed by the risen Lord to the disciples. Much had been made of this by biblical critics. One peculiar feature of the *Washington Codex* attracted immediate attention from scholars. It contained the disputed last twelve verses of Mark's gospel. That enabled scholars to come to terms with the omission from *Sinaiticus*. *Sinaiticus* omitted the last few verses of Mark; *Vaticanus* omitted the latter part of the letter to the Hebrews. *Both were contained in the Washington Codex.* Many scholars began to put the omissions down to human fallibility or fatigue. Certainly significance ceased to be attached to them.

The Chester-Beatty collection, with the *Washington Codex*, 'between them carried back the textual tradition of the New Testament for a full century . . .', stated Sir Frederic Kenyon in 1948. 'The Chester-Beatty papyri have therefore strengthened very materially the basis – already very strong – of our confidence in the text of the New Testament as it has come down to us.'[8]

The oldest fragment of all

One final dramatic discovery was to be made in the battle for the New Testament. It would appear that the discovery was made as early as 1920, but it was not until 1936 when it was brought to Britain and that experts pronounced on exactly what it was.

The confusion is not too surprising. The oldest of all biblical fragments – now to be found in the John Rylands University Library, Manchester – was simply a torn fragment which for centuries helped to wrap up an Egyptian mummy. Some of the fragments date from the second century *before* Christ and contain verses in Hebrew from Deuteronomy. But the oldest fragment of the *New* Testament, now known as 'the Rylands fragment', dates from the first half of the second century AD. The fragment of papyrus is no bigger than a man's hand and, on both sides, contains verses from the eighteenth chapter of John's gospel (verses 31-33, 37, 38).

The nineteenth-century critics had been unanimous in assigning the gospel of John to a very late date indeed, and in asserting that John's authorship of it was an impossibility. The importance of the Rylands fragment to papyrological experts is that it was written in the first half of the second century, *in other words shortly after John's death (in or around AD100)*. Hence Christian scholars have reason to be grateful to the Egyptian hands who used this fragment of the gospel to help mummify a body, thus keeping the fragment as well as the body in conditions which would enable both to survive the centuries. The fragment suffices to prove that a manuscript of John's gospel was in circulation in provincial Egypt, where it was found, about the period AD130-150. Commenting on this, Sir Frederic Kenyon states: 'Allowing even a minimum time for the circulation of the work from its place of origin, this would throw back the date of composition so near to the traditional date in the last decade of the first century that there is no longer any reason to question the validity of the tradition.' The tradition being, of course, that John wrote the gospel that bears his name and that he did so in the late 90s of the first century.

In the same year in which the significance of the Rylands fragment was first appreciated, Dr H. I. Bell and Mr T. C. Skeat bought three leaves of papyrus codex for the British Museum. The three leaves contained portions of a life of Christ which, though not drawn from any of the four gospels, did not differ from them. The leaves also contained excerpts from each of the four gospels.

The quotations from John's gospel (5:39, 45; 9:29; 7:30; 10:39) are accepted as further proof of the traditional date of John's gospel and of his authorship of it. The three leaves of papyrus codex, like the Rylands fragment, are dated in the first half of the second century.[9]

As he reviewed, in 1948, the discovery of biblical manuscripts in the previous half century, Sir Frederic Kenyon believed that the contentions of the critical school of Baur and van Manen had been 'shattered to pieces'.

The time had come, he said, to reassess the value of the criticism of Scripture which had been characteristic of the previous 150 years with regard to 'the authenticity and authority of the books of which the Bible is composed'. Recent discoveries, said Kenyon, had enhanced the position of the conservative Bible student 'very materially'. It was time 'to shake off the excessive scepticism characteristic of much biblical scholarship in the latter part of the nineteenth century, and to restore confidence in the Bible as a guide to truth and a basis for the conduct of life.'[10]

The higher critics of the nineteenth century had challenged Christian scholarship to provide 'the merest fragment' of a manuscript dated from between the first and the fourth centuries. In making their challenge they had been certain that 'the gap' between the time when Christians believed that the New Testament books had been completed (*circa* AD100) and AD300-350 (the date of the *Codex Sinaiticus*) would never be bridged.

From the perspective of the mid-twentieth century it appeared that their demand for 'the merest fragment' had been but a modest one. *They had had a veritable avalanche of fragments, plus whole libraries of papyri and even more codices.* No one could challenge Kenyon's conclusion: 'A large part of the gap between the original writers and the earliest manuscripts which we possess has thus been filled.'[11]

Against immense odds and all the probabilities, the battle for the New Testament had been won. And it had been a rout.

The manuscript evidence for the authenticity of the New Testament is far, far in excess of that which can be marshalled for any other document of antiquity. Over 5,300 Greek manuscripts of the New Testament, 8,000 Latin Vulgate and more than 9,300 manuscripts of other early versions are now available. This contrasts with the next most authenticated work of ancient times: Homer's *Iliad*. Of Homer's *Iliad* 643 manuscripts survive.

And the variations between the thousands of ancient New Testament manuscripts? Who better than Professors B. F. Westcott and F. J. A. Hort, who spent forty years studying them, to speak on the subject:

'If comparative trivialities such as change of order, the insertion or omission of the article with proper names, and the like are set aside, the words in our opinion subject to doubt can hardly amount to more than a thousandth part of the New Testament.'[12]

References
[1] Sir Frederic Kenyon, *The Bible and Modern Scholarship*, pages 4-8.
[2] Ibid, pages 16-23; Sir Frederic Kenyon, *The Story of the Bible*, pages 1-110.
[3] Ibid, page 95.
[4] Sir Frederic Kenyon, *The Bible and Modern Scholarship*, pages 16, 17.
[5] Sir Frederic Kenyon, *The Story of the Bible*, pages 96, 97.
[6] Ibid.
[7] Ibid, pages 113-116.
[8] Sir Frederic Kenyon, *The Bible and Modern Scholarship*, pages 18-21.
[9] Ibid, pages 21-23. Kenyon adduces further compelling evidence for John's authorship of the gospel that bears his name. See pages 23-26.
[10] Ibid, pages vii, 23.
[11] Sir Frederic Kenyon, *The Story of the Bible*, page 117.
[12] B. F. Westcott and F. J. A. Hort, *The New Testament in the Original Greek*, volume 1, page 2.

3

The Story of the English Bible

The Bible and the dawn of Christianity

The front runners of Christianity carried with them an unshakable faith in the fact of the resurrection. Wherever they went they also carried with them the Old Testament Scriptures from which to demonstrate that all had been foretold. The substance of the sermons recorded in the book of Acts and of the theological arguments of Paul, Peter, James and John in their letters, was Old Testament Scripture. Every broad acre and tiny fleck of messianic prophecy had been fulfilled in the life of Jesus.

Among Christianity's frontiersmen: translators

As Christianity's first frontiersmen pressed further and further, they discovered that the Hebrew Scriptures, which had served as their evangelistic text with the Jews, and the Scriptures in Greek, which had enabled them to touch base with both Jews and Gentiles, were ceasing to be adequate. They were encountering groups capable of understanding neither language.

Hence, perhaps by the end of the first century, certainly in the second century, the translation of the Scriptures – both testaments – followed immediately on the introduction of Christianity to a nation with a new language. When the gospel spread east, a Syriac New Testament was one of the first monuments to its power. When it spread west, a Latin translation. Ulfilas, the second bishop of the Goths, gave them the Scriptures in their own language. Miesrob, who framed the Armenian alphabet, also translated the Armenian Bible.[1]

The New Testament was translated into Syriac and Latin by about AD150 and into Egyptian by about AD200. Papyri of those early translations are extant. They are copies directly 'descended' from those original translations. As language scholars scrutinise the Syrian, Egyptian and Latin texts, they discover the exact Greek text which the translator was working from. Hence it is possible to know from the Syriac, Latin and Egyptian translations what words were found in the Greek manuscript which had been extant between AD100 and 150. That has been another, independent line, along which it has been possible to recover the original texts of our Bible.[2]

The Syrian version has opened up even more exciting lines of enquiry. Syriac was not just the language of Mesopotamia and Syria but, with variations in dialect, one of the everyday languages of Palestine in the days of Jesus. The Syriac translation from the Greek was undertaken by Tatian (born *circa* 110; died *circa* 165). Such a large proportion of Tarian's Syriac Bible was discovered in the Vatican library that it was possible in 1888 to publish it. This has led scholars excitingly close, not only to the Greek text of the gospels at the time, but to the direct speech of the first three-and-a-half decades of the Christian era.[3]

The Vulgate

The importance of Rome, the arrival of Christianity there, and the spread of Christianity in countries conquered by Rome, made the Latin Bible one of vital importance. The first translation is referred to as 'the Old Latin'. But this was to be superseded by Jerome's Latin Vulgate, following Constantine's Christianisation of the Roman Empire.

'The Old Latin' translation, made around AD150, is valuable evidence – perhaps *the* most valuable evidence – of the condition of the New Testament 'in the earliest times'.[4] It is seen by scholars as the last link in the chain from our modern New Testaments to the quill pens of the apostles who wrote the New Testament's original twenty-seven books.

It was in its Latin form that the Bible arrived in the British Isles. The British Isles were to produce, however, their own breed of champions of the cross. And these champions, so distant from the home of Latin, were to adapt biblical precepts in their own way and teach them in the vernaculars of the races of these distant isles. Nevertheless, it would take a thousand years of conquest and internal strife before the southern portion of these islands we call Britain would produce a complete written Bible in the language then spoken by the mass of the people.

References:
[1] B. F. Westcott, *A General View of the History of the English Bible* (third edition), page 3.
[2] Sir Frederic Kenyon, *Our Bible and the Ancient Manuscripts*, page 155.
[3] Ibid, pages 156-159.
[4] Ibid, pages 170, 171.

Britain's first Bibles

We do not know exactly when the Bible came to Britain or who brought it. We do not know *exactly* when Christianity arrived, except that it was long before Augustine put ashore off Kent in AD597.

There were Celtic Christians long before Augustine. They were known for their commitment to the Scriptures. Bede (*circa* 672-735) believed that during the persecution associated with the name of the Emperor Diocletian (284-305) 'faithful Christians' in Britain had suffered.[1] Gildas, another historian of the Britons, affirms that at the time of Diocletian's onslaught on the Bible, when the inscription '*Extincto nomine Christianorum*' (the name of Christianity has been destroyed) was put over the ashes of a codex of the Bible, 'parts of the Scriptures were burnt in the streets of British towns'.[2]

Certainly three representatives from Britain attended the Council of Arles in 314. By then Constantine reigned and Christianity was a favoured religion. As previously stated, in 332 the Emperor commissioned from Bishop Eusebius of Caesarea fifty copies of the Scriptures (two of which may well be extant in the *Codex Sinaiticus* and the *Codex Vaticanus*).

The Bible from Bethlehem

But these were Greek Bibles, and Britain's first Bibles were Latin. To be exact: 'Old Latin'. In 382 Pope Damasus commissioned Jerome (*circa* 347-420) to produce a more accurate, authoritative Latin Bible. Jerome had studied Greek and Hebrew, but was by instinct conservative. Hence the New Testament he set down was merely a revision of the existing Latin translation. There is some evidence that he had recourse to the Greek manuscripts, but alterations were made only when he considered them strictly necessary. By contrast his Old Testament was 'an altogether new translation from the Hebrew'.[3] His work was completed about 404, had taken twenty years and had been accomplished in Bethlehem.

Jerome's Bible became known as the *Vulgate*. For a thousand years it was the adopted Bible of Western Christendom. Syrians, Egyptians, Armenians and Persians had their own vernacular Bibles. But Western Europe was content with one Bible in an international language. No great library was without a manuscript. It was copied innumerable times and hence there were innumerable tiny variations from one manuscript to the next. Eight thousand manuscripts are still extant. During the Vulgate's thousand-year reign, all books were written in Latin. Latin was the language of the monasteries, which were the chief centres of learning, and all educated men spoke Latin.

The Celtic Church

But if a Latin speaker could be equally at home in Italy, Gaul or southern Britain, there were fringes — Ireland and northern Britain — where Latin culture was not at home, and Christianity developed a different coloration.

The century before Augustine landed in Kent was a glorious period in the history of the Irish Church. That was thanks largely to Patrick. Having embraced Christianity, he took ship to Ireland and began to evangelise the land where he had once been a slave. Patrick's preaching came to the notice of the first of the 'High Kings' of Ireland. Soon the King's son, Conall, was baptised by Patrick. Thousands followed his lead. Conall's great-grandson Columba was to be the missionary of the Celtic Church to the mainland. Iona was his missionary base.

The Celtic Church believed in the primacy of Scripture. Finding some ideas in the belief and practice of the Roman Church unscriptural, Celtic Christians rejected them. In Rome they spoke of 'the schismatic Celts', and the Pope originated the plan to send Augustine to 'correct the obstinate' Celtic Christians.[4]

The death of Columba and the arrival of Augustine occurred within twelve months of each other. Among the Saxons south of the Thames, Augustine encountered considerable resistance to his attempts to impose Roman order; and there was even more resistance further north.[5] But even this resistance was minimal by comparison with that encountered within the Northumbrian kingdom north of the Humber.[6] There the ecclesiastical centre was Lindisfarne. Lindisfarne's bishop was Aidan, a disciple of Columba, who had been invited to evangelise Northumbria by King Oswald.[7]

The confrontation between the Celtic Church and the Roman order introduced by Augustine took place at the Council of Whitby in 664. The Roman model triumphed. 'The Scots Bishop Colman left Britain,' reports Bede, 'taking with him the Scots he had collected at Lindisfarne, together with about thirty English whom he had likewise trained in the monastic life.'[8] They found another retreat off the coast of Ireland.

Some have viewed the decision at the Council of Whitby as a setback for the Bible and for Bible-based Christianity.

The Lindisfarne gospels

But Lindisfarne and the Church it represented had carved for itself an abiding place in the history of the English Bible. There the Lindisfarne gospels were produced. These superbly illuminated manuscripts, now in the British Museum, are the finest artefacts still remaining of the Celtic Church. They were produced in honour of St Cuthbert who had died in 687. 'The main text is that of the Latin Vulgate; but between the lines a later hand has written a paraphrase of the Latin into the primitive English we commonly call Anglo-Saxon.'[9]

Caedmon of Whitby

A further significant development in the history of the English Bible was to take place at Whitby. A barrier of language separated the peoples of Britain from the Latin Vulgate of Jerome. The first effort to break it down was made by Caedmon in the cloisters of Whitby Abbey just five years after the famous Council.

Caedmon – according to Bede, 'well advanced in years'[10] – arrived at Whitby's Abbey from the agricultural land nearby. He had discovered a gift for poetry and music, apparently by accident. He humbly reported to the authorities at the Abbey that he had received this new gift. 'All of them agreed that Caedmon's gift had been given him by our Lord,' writes Bede. 'And they explained to him a passage of scriptural history or doctrine and asked him to render it into verse if he could. He promised to do this, and returned next morning with excellent verses as they had ordered him.' Thus Caedmon became the humblest of the Abbey's lay brothers.

'He sang of the creation of the world, the origin of the human race, and the whole story of Genesis. He sang of Israel's exodus from Egypt, the entry into the Promised Land. . . .'[11] The important thing was that he did all this in Anglo-Saxon, the language of the common people, not in Latin, the language of the learned. Caedmon had made the first-known attempt at a paraphrase of the Bible – actually, the Bible's best-known stories – in the vernacular.

The 229-page Caedmon manuscript is still to be found in the Bodleian Library, Oxford. Critical examination of the manuscript has brought to light evidence of vigorous editing. Nevertheless, there can be no doubt that the original work was that of the eloquent cowherd who turned up at Whitby Abbey one bright morning, announced his God-given gift and was admitted by Abbess Hilda. That was in 670. He died in the Abbey precincts just ten years later.

Aldhelm and Bede

Aldhelm, Bishop of Sherborn, who died in 709, has the distinction of being the first translator of a part of the Bible into the native tongue of England. A manuscript of the Psalms in Anglo-Saxon has been preserved in Paris. This is thought to have been Aldhelm's work.[12]

Bede, born in 674, studied Latin, Greek and Hebrew and is

known as the author of *History of the English Church and People*. At the monastery in Jarrow he also translated what he considered to be the essentials of the Christian faith into the language of the people.[13] These essentials included the Apostles' Creed and the Lord's Prayer. Towards the end of his life Bede also embarked upon a translation of the gospel of John. He completed the translation on his death bed.

King Alfred the translator

The fourth link in the chain – Caedmon, Aldhelm and Bede – takes us by surprise: King Alfred the Great.

Alfred became King of Wessex at 22 in AD865, and ruled the kingdom until his death at the age of 50. Much of his reign was spent in the task of containing the Danish invasion.

But Alfred was a scholar. Aware that the Emperor Charlemagne had instigated a revision of the Vulgate in the early ninth century (a task ignored by the Church itself until the sixteenth century), Alfred turned his attention towards translating parts of the Vulgate into the common tongue. While Vikings burned their way across England, leaving the great libraries and monasteries in ashes, Alfred was working on a new system of law. He prefixed this with a translation, of the Ten Commandments and other extracts from the law of Moses. In addition he 'translated or caused to be translated, several parts of the Bible'.[14] Like Bede, he was engaged in translation at the time of his death; in Alfred's case it was the book of Psalms.

An age of change and disorder

In the century and a half before the Norman Conquest of 1066, there was a marked decline in the level of scholarship among the priesthood. Not only were the common people unable to understand the Latin of the Vulgate Bible, but a major proportion of the clergy did not understand it either.

That accounts for the appearance of *glosses* in that period. Glosses were word-for-word translations into early English written between the lines of Latin manuscripts. The first-known example was the Lindisfarne gospel. But glosses did not become extremely common until the tenth century. Glosses of the gospels dating from around 950 are to be found in Oxford and at the British Museum. They must have been of value to priests when instructing their congregations.

Work on glosses led, naturally, to renewed interest in producing an actual translation, independent of the Latin text. A complete English translation of the gospels appeared in the tenth century, apparently for public use. Six copies are extant. The earliest – in the library of Corpus Christi College, Cambridge – was the work of Elfric of Bath and has been dated around AD1000. There is evidence that a large part of the Old Testament was translated by someone else at about the same time.[15]

The Norman Conquest effectively halted the literary development of the English people for three centuries. The Anglo-Saxon gospels dropped out of use. The common people's access to much of the Bible was provided by crude rhyming paraphrases.

But the fourteenth century brought with it great changes.

There was the Black Death of 1348-49 in which one-third of the population died. The same period, 1344-50, brought famine and war. Developments like these predisposed men to interpret events in prophetic and millenarian terms.

Similar upheavals in France led to the *Jacquerie* of 1358 – and a preoccupation with matters apocalyptic. It was 'back to the Bible' time. The French first produced a revised edition of the Vulgate, then the first complete version of the Bible in French.

The power of the Papacy was in decline. Corruption permeated the higher clergy. The Church became a subject for satire and vilification in England. Corruption and decline reached the monasteries.

Corruption in the Church was paralleled by restlessness among the masses. English culture was reasserted. The movement began which led to the work of Langland and Chaucer.

There was a dim awareness that Christendom was being menaced to the east and south by the forces of Islam.

In England 'men turned with intense longing to the Bible.'[16]

A corrupt Church. Society in turmoil. The dimly understood menace to Christendom itself. The background was in place against which John Wyclif made his great contribution to the

history of the English Bible and of the English Church.

References:
[1] Bede, *A History of the English Church and People* (Penguin Classics), page 48; on the Celtic Church see the author's *The Celtic Connection* (Autumn House).

[2] Cited Charles Gulston, *No Greater Heritage*, page 17.

[3] Sir Frederic Kenyon, *Our Bible and the Ancient Manuscripts*, page 174.

[4] Bede, *op cit*, pages 146-148. The beliefs of the Celtic Church are discussed in detail by Leslie Hardinge in *The Celtic Church in Britain* (SPCK). This book represents a distillation of Dr Hardinge's PhD thesis (University of London).

[5] Bede, *op cit*, pages 68-107.

[6] Ibid, page 107.

[7] Ibid, page 144.

[8] Ibid, pages 185-192, 193, 213; Sir Frederic Kenyon, *op cit*, page 183.

[9] Kenyon, *op cit*, page 184.

[10] Bede, *op cit*, page 251.

[11] Ibid, page 252.

[12] Kenyon, *op cit*, page 195; B. F. Westcott, *A General View of the History of the English Bible* (third edition), page 4.

[13] Kenyon, *op cit*, page 195; Charles Gulston, *op cit*, pages 35-40.

[14] Kenyon, *op cit*, page 196; Westcott, *op cit*, page 5.

[15] Kenyon, *op cit*, pages 197-199; Westcott, *op cit*, page 6; Gulston, *op cit*, pages 53-72.

[16] Westcott, *op cit*, page 11.

Two recent histories of the English Bible: Benson Bobrick, *The Making of the English Bible* (Phoenix). Alister McGrath, *In the Beginning: The Story of the King James Bible and How It Changed a Nation, a Language and a Culture* (Hodder and Stoughton)

The Bible for the people

A bleak churchyard in Lutterworth, Leicestershire. A dark, cold day at the dawn of 1385. A small group of figures, some in cassocks of black or russet, and others with threadbare shawls pulled tightly around their shoulders, huddled together over an open grave. There was a flurry of words in Latin as the coffin was lowered. John Wyclif was safe at last from his enemies.

Wyclif had died on the last day of 1384. A few years after the icy day of his burial, rude hands were to unearth his coffin, burn its contents and, at the orders of the Bishop of Lincoln, scatter his ashes into the River Swift.

The making of Wyclif

Wyclif's twin crimes had been to expose the corruption of the Church of his day and, with a group of scholars, to translate Jerome's 1,000-year-old Latin Bible into English.

John of Wyclif had been born in the village of Wyclif around 1320. The village, like the nearby town of Barnard Castle, clings to the banks of the River Tees. He was the son of the lord of the manor.

It appears that John Wyclif left his home village at 14. His older brother was content to remain as parish priest.

John Wyclif became an undergraduate at Balliol College, Oxford and, much later, was elected Master of his college. In those days he distinguished himself as a scholar and made some prominent friends, among them John of Gaunt, the King's son. There is a record of his having been appointed chaplain to the

King and of his having had the degree of Doctor of Divinity conferred upon him.

For the future, however, his friendship with John of Gaunt, who exercised feudal dominion over the northlands, was to prove a matter of life and death to him. John of Gaunt was based in the castle at Richmond, not far from the place of Wyclif's birth. But his power extended as far south as the villages of Fillingham (Lincolnshire), and Lutterworth (Leicestershire), where Wyclif was to be priest, as well as to Oxford where, in practice, he was to spend the greater part of his working life.

Wyclif's only excursion outside his own country, in 1374, was to be in the company of John of Gaunt. Both men visited Bruges in Flanders. John of Gaunt was there to negotiate peace with the French. John of Wyclif was part of an investigative commission appointed by Parliament to enquire into the number of ecclesiastical benefices in England held by foreigners. Wyclif's disillusionment with the Church and the papacy dates from his visit to Bruges. From Bruges he emerged a reformer. Soon he would be a marked man and the target of papal bulls. Only John of Gaunt's intervention enabled him to die peacefully.

Though spending the greater part of his time at Oxford until the spring of 1381, Wyclif was appointed to the living at Fillingham in 1361. It was at Fillingham that his feud with the mendicant friars began. The mendicants, who had set out to reform the monastic system, had, by this time, become more corrupt than the system they had set out to change. It is likely that it was from his battle with the mendicants that Wyclif conceived the idea of translating the Bible, to reveal to his parishioners the fraud and greed of the mendicants and the system they represented.

Public controversies

Wyclif's middle life was marked by his involvement in public controversies. The massive financial cost of the protracted wars with France, the demands for money from the papacy, and the ostentatious wealth of the high dignitaries of the Church who supported papal claims, shuddered discontent through English society. Wyclif's treatises and sermons against these disorders did not, in themselves, mark him out as a front-rank reformer. What *did* make him stand out were his aristocratic connections and the fact that Oxford afforded him a great many public platforms from which to preach. His influence was such that by 1371 he was in the forefront of religious and social disturbance.

Oxford supported John Wyclif until 1380 when his attacks made him an embarrassment. Even John of Gaunt, who had his own reasons for wishing to humiliate the Church, felt obliged to back off towards the end.

In his treatise *Objections to the Friars*, Wyclif argued powerfully against the sale of indulgences, thus anticipating Luther by one-and-a-half centuries.

The very causes that attracted to him the hostility of Church authorities ensured Wyclif a following among the common people. Soon he was perceived as their champion. In the last five years of his life he attracted a considerable following of 'poor priests'. These 'Lollards' went about preaching to the common people.[1]

Three papal bulls were soon chasing Wyclif. One was sent to the Archbishop of Canterbury, another to the University of Oxford, and the third to the King. All indicted the Rector of Lutterworth, John Wyclif, for 'most wicked and damnable heresies'. In fact the bishops had instituted proceedings before the papal bulls had arrived. In February 1377 Wyclif was ordered to appear in Our Lady's Chapel in St Paul's to face the consequences of his words and deeds.

Wyclif's reception by the populace in London must have done much to lift his spirits. It was only with the greatest difficulty that he, with his two patrons – John of Gaunt, Duke of Lancaster; and Lord Percy, Earl Marshal of England – could force their way through the massive throng surrounding St Paul's.

It was made very clear to both Wyclif and his protectors that he was standing trial.

In no time the trial had to be abandoned.

The mob burst in. Uproar ensued.

Wyclif did not wait for another hearing but returned to Oxford.

Before many months passed the fact of his popular standing was to become apparent again. His arguments enabled parliament to end the outflow of revenue to the Papacy.

But the bishops were still more determined to bring the reformer to book after their experience at St Paul's. This time Wyclif was summoned to Lambeth Palace. He went alone; his excursions into 'heresy' were embarrassing even John of Gaunt. But they were not embarrassing the mob who, once again, were out in force in favour of their champion. The chapel where he was tried was chock-full. Before proceedings were long under way an emissary arrived from court. He carried a warrant for safe conduct signed by the Queen Mother. It forbade any sentence being passed on Wyclif.

The bishops knew when they were beaten.

The mob was jubilant as Wyclif walked triumphantly to freedom.

Back in Lutterworth he wrote and published *On the Schism of the Popes* in which he openly stated his opposition to papal authority. In a second pamphlet *On the Truth and Meaning of Scripture* he argued the case for the supremacy of Scripture in matters of doctrine.

Wyclif the translator

Doubt remains as to the exact date when Wyclif began his Bible translation. However, it is certain that by the time of the papal schism – 1378 – it was well under way.

At the height of the Reformation controversy of the sixteenth century, Sir Thomas More, in controversy with William Tyndale, would say that he had seen an English Bible that predated Wyclif's. The Catholic scholar *might* have been referring to a partial translation undertaken by Richard Rolle who died in 1349. More likely, however, More was unaware that *two* translations were associated with the name of John Wyclif. If this were the case, clearly he had seen the older one.

Wyclif began by translating the last book in the Scriptures: Revelation. That was followed by a 'Harmony of the Gospels': a single life of Christ made from an intelligent integration of material from all four gospel accounts.

Wyclif's first New Testament was finished in 1380; in 1384 the whole Bible was completed. That came to be known as 'the earlier Wycliffite Bible'. Constantly in touch with both Oxford and London, Wyclif undertook his work of translation from Latin to English at Lutterworth. Without doubt he had the assistance of other scholars. Even the New Testament was not entirely his own work, and the greater part of the Old Testament was certainly translated by Nicholas Hereford, a colleague and friend from Oxford.

At that stage Wyclif seems to have been beyond the reach of the ecclesiastical authorities. Hereford was not. In 1382 he was summoned to London. He was excommunicated. To save his life he fled to the Continent.

At the time of Hereford's flight the Old Testament was not quite complete. One of Wyclif's assistants brought it to completion. Hence the entire Bible had been finished just prior to Wyclif's death at the end of 1384.

A study of the first 'Wycliffite' Bible made it obvious where Wyclif's translation left off and Hereford's translation began. Hereford used a pedantic, translator's English. Wyclif's style, by contrast, was free and colloquial. 'There can be no doubt,' writes Sir Frederic Kenyon, 'that he had in his mind the common people, for whom his version was especially intended.'[2]

The second 'Wycliffite' Bible made its appearance after his death. It represented a revision of the earlier translation. This later Bible was completed in 1388. It is generally assumed that John Purvey, one of Wyclif's closest friends, undertook the entire work of revision. About 170 copies of this version are still extant.

Neither 'Wycliffite' Bible was written with any ornamentation. The copies were essentially prepared for private use only. The Wycliffite Bibles were aimed at those who could not read Latin. There was never any thought that it would supplant the Vulgate for scholarly use. The original biblical languages, Greek and Hebrew, were not consulted.

Though every attempt was made by the bishops to impound and burn Wyclif's Bibles, they continued to be copied throughout the fifteenth century. Wyclif's reforming views also survived him by many years. Indeed, following his death, the Poor Preachers (or Lollards) were even more active than before. Wyclif's ideas sparked other reforming movements elsewhere; both Jerome of Prague and John Huss of Bohemia acknowledged their indebtedness to the English reformer.

Renaissance

In the mid-fifteenth century two events occurred, the effects of which would revolutionise the history of the Bible. First, in May 1453 the Turks stormed Constantinople. Second, in November 1454 the first dated product of the printing press emerged.

The fall of the Eastern Empire forced West many scholars learned in both Greek and Hebrew. Both languages were almost forgotten in Western Europe. As the Constantinople scholars settled in Italy and elsewhere they fuelled the Renaissance spirit of enquiry and an enthusiasm to read the classics – including the Bible – in their original languages. Soon in universities in Italy, Flanders and England, Greek and Hebrew were being revived. The way was opened up for the appearance of accurate vernacular Bibles, based on the oldest available manuscripts in the original biblical languages.

Johann Gutenberg of Mainz (*circa* 1398-1468) is credited with the invention of printing. By August 1456 he had published his first Bible: Jerome's Latin Vulgate.

The invention of printing not only made possible the propagation of the Scriptures, but helped to ensure their accuracy. The realisation of Wyclif's vision was within prospect: the Bible accessible to every man.

The earliest printed vernacular Bibles predated the Reformation. A German Bible was printed at Strasburg in 1466. Eighteen others were to be published before the first of Luther's translations appeared in 1522. An Italian Bible was printed in Venice in 1471, a Dutch Bible in 1477, a French Bible at Lyons in 1478 and another about 1487. Caxton's *Golden Legend*, published in 1483, was the nearest England came to a printed vernacular Bible during the fifteenth century; it included a part of the Bible narrative in English. It did not, however, eclipse the work of John Wyclif.

The eve of Reformation

John Wyclif and his followers had anticipated many of the key doctrines of the Reformation 150 years before it occurred. The 'obstinate North Country mind endowed with the subtleties of the Oxford schools'[3] had established a principle which became more and more widely accepted: an accessible Bible as the only way to, and foundation of, truth. Wyclif also placed squarely on the shoulders of the temporal rulers the responsibility for reforming the Church. Within a few years of his death his doctrines developed 'a widespread appeal among townsmen, merchants, gentry and even among some of the lower clergy'.[4]

In the course of the fifteenth century, persecution forced Lollardy underground. During his lifetime Wyclif had powerful protectors. Following his death those protectors distanced themselves from the movement to which he had given rise. Nevertheless, the 'inspiration' of English heresy 'was overwhelmingly Wyclif, at least until about 1530'.[5] A steady stream of Lollards and Lollard Bibles was being burned until the eve of the English Reformation.[6]

References:
[1] K. B. McFarlane, *Wyclif and English Nonconformity*, pages 78, 79.
[2] Sir Frederic Kenyon, *Our Bible and the Ancient Manuscripts*, page 204.
[3] A. G. Dickens, *The English Reformation*, page 41.
[4] Ibid, page 42.
[5] Ibid, page 47.
[6] Ibid, pages 48-62.

Note
Benson Bobrick, *The Making of the English Bible*, has an excellent chapter on Wyclif, 'The Morning Star'.

Outlawed!

What made Bible translation both imperative and controversial was the Reformation.

Reformers believed that the most effective way to destroy the authority of the Roman Church was to give the people a Bible they could read for themselves. In Germany – the birthplace of the Reformation movement – a popular version was prepared by Luther with the connivance of the local Prince. In England, Bible translation would be undertaken in the face of the opposition of both Church *and* Prince. It would ultimately be the work of many hands. But one above all: William Tyndale.

A forbidden book

More than a century earlier (in 1408), and as a reaction to the popularity of the Wyclif Bible, a prohibition by the authorities had ordained 'that no one henceforth on his own authority [shall] translate any text of Holy Scripture into English'. It also reinforced the illegality of Wyclif's version.

Wyclif had given the English a taste for Scripture that neither prohibition nor time diminished. However, Wyclif's Bible, with the passage of time, had acquired two handicaps. One, because it came via the Latin, it was inaccurate. Two, because of its illegality, it had never been printed. The Reformation movement made necessary a new English translation that would harness Renaissance knowledge and technology.

What gave William Tyndale the text from which to translate was a Greek New Testament published in 1516 by Renaissance scholar Erasmus.

But what gave him the vision?

The story of Tyndale has all the ingredients of a spy thriller. One man's passion for a forbidden book. Agents and double agents. Kings, popes and cardinals. Constant danger and pursuit. Hairbreadth escapes under cover of darkness. Villains and traitors. And a hero with endless courage.

Decision in the great hall

Tyndale was born in Gloucestershire. Despite the role that life made him play, he was, by instinct, a modest, quiet scholar. After spending five years at Oxford and three at Cambridge he left university and directed his footsteps to a village nestling in the slopes of the Cotswold hills, near his place of birth. He spent the next eighteen months in the employment of the squire of Little Sodbury, Sir John Walsh. He worked as tutor to the squire's children. It was in the great hall of the manor house at Little Sodbury that his destiny was decided.

Sir John was a local dignitary. The great hall of his manor house saw many a distinguished guest. In the long winter evenings all kinds of important men would sit at Sir John's long oak table, including the odd bishop. Those important men discussed the great issues of the day. The revolutionary preaching of Luther of Wittenberg was the centre of the controversy.

As an educated man Tyndale took part in their discussions. Indeed, he was often at the heart of the debate. On religious issues he tended to disagree with the other guests. He knew the Bible so well that he often beat them down with arguments.

On one memorable evening when the discussion was particularly heated, one scholar, thus beaten down, shouted: 'We had better be without God's laws than the Pope's!' In reply, slowly and deliberately, Tyndale uttered the fateful words: 'I defy the Pope and all his laws. If God spare my life, ere many years I will cause the boy who drives the plough to know more about the Scriptures than you do!'

To London

A few days later Tyndale had his first brush with the authorities. He had been preaching at College Green, Bristol, and fallen foul of the local priests. Before a local court he was charged with heresy. To fulfil his ambition of translating the New Testament into English and realising that he could not remain a free man for long in that part of the country, Tyndale set out on his long trek to distant London.

London had printing presses. It also had the advantage, Tyndale believed, of an enlightened bishop. Cuthbert Tunstall was a scholar and a friend of Erasmus. 'Then thought I, if I might come to this man's service, I were happy,' wrote Tyndale later. 'So I gat me to London.'

Tyndale arrived in the mid-summer of 1523. In his pocket he carried a letter of introduction from Sir John Walsh to the Controller of the Royal household. In his heart he carried the hope that somehow an interview with Bishop Tunstall would be arranged and his support secured for his plan to translate the New Testament, and in the end the whole Bible, into the English current at the time. The financial and moral backing of the Bishop of London could make or break his plans.

No room in all England!

After many weeks he obtained an interview with the Bishop. He entered the courtyard of the Bishop's palace and pulled the huge bell. Soon he was seated in the audience chamber. The light of the setting sun streamed in through the latticed windows, making chequered the sombre garb of the Bishop of London. Soon the sun was to set for ever on Tyndale's fortunes in England.

The Bishop did not say much. His favour at court was good. The project was risky. From the moment he entered the Bishop's chamber Tyndale knew his hopes were dashed. In Germany Martin Luther, having produced a German Bible, was leading the attack on the Catholic Church. The Bishop was afraid that Tyndale aimed to do the same in England. And so, wrote Tyndale: 'My lord answered me that his house was full, and advised me to seek in London, where he said I could not lack service.' Tunstall was, Tyndale decided, 'a ducking hypocrite, made to dissemble'.

As the shadows of night deepened he trudged the darkened streets, his hopes and dreams blasted. The money given him by Sir John was spent. He was penniless. But Tyndale believed that God had given him a task to do. Hence he ventured to believe that God would give him the means to do it. That he found in the home of a rich cloth merchant of Barking, Humphrey Monmouth, a travelled and generous-hearted man.

Monmouth took Tyndale in after he had heard him preach. Later he would testify: 'I took him into my house half a year; and there he lived like a good priest. . . . He studied most part of the day and of the night at his book.'

Tyndale was, in fact, working on the first draft of his New Testament. But he knew that if his work were ever to be published he must seek another land. In the house of Monmouth he met many wealthy merchants who were to provide vital assistance in future days. They were part of the international world of Lutheranism and, according to A. G. Dickens, 'were certainly linked with men of Lollard background'. In one of their ships he was soon leaving the shores of England behind. If his work of translation were ever to be completed and published he must seek other, more congenial shores. In May 1524 he sailed for Hamburg, never to return.

'Not only was there no room in my Lord of London's palace to translate the Scriptures,' he said, 'but there was no room in all England.'

Under cover

After the merchantman docked at Hamburg, mystery covers Tyndale's movements. His story takes on even more the atmosphere of a modern spy thriller – secret comings and goings, undercover meetings, narrow escapes, spies, agents and a traitor within the gates. Tyndale and his accomplices were in constant fear of detection and of their lives. Strange, and all the stranger when one considers what they were trying to do – translate and publish an English Bible.

Sources hostile to Tyndale implied that he matriculated at the University of Wittenberg on 27 May 1524. Despite the fact that the motive behind that allegation was to create an association between Tyndale and Luther, Wittenberg was the obvious place to go. Luther's German Bible had already been published. Wittenberg's Professor of Greek was Philip Melanchthon, and its Professor of Hebrew, Aurogallus. While Tyndale already had a scholar's knowledge of both languages and at least part of an English New Testament in manuscript form, the advice of such scholars and access to their libraries would have been of tremendous help. Certainly Tyndale would have found at Wittenberg an atmosphere suitable for the work of translation.

While at Wittenberg, he employed runaway friar William Roye as a secretary and 'manager'. On Tyndale's own description, Roye was something of a rascal. But his cunning was to prove an asset.

By the spring of 1525 the New Testament had been translated into English. The first part of the job was done. Now for the second part: Where should it be printed and who should print it? Anything coming from Wittenberg was suspect. Cologne, on the other hand, had many printers and was in a far better position for shipping the printed works to England. Around the hearth of Humphrey Monmouth in Barking, Tyndale had hatched a plan with sympathetic merchants. His Bibles, packed in bales of cloth and other merchandise, would be smuggled into England. Cologne was ideal for putting this plan into action.

In August 1525 he arrived in Cologne, still accompanied by his useful, if not altogether honest, friend Roye. In that city of spires and turrets, sloping down to the Rhine, they had little difficulty in contacting a printer. Peter Quentel was willing to undertake the venture in the strictest secrecy. Soon the type was set up, and preparation was made to print 3,000 copies.

The traitor

During this period of preparation Tyndale had been in a constant state of tension. This was a vital stage. All that was required was for one person to report to the authorities and life and labours would be lost. News was coming through from England of a new spate of burnings. The Emperor Charles V was eager to stamp out heresy in Germany. His agents were everywhere. It was a desperate gamble. Would it pay off? Hearts thumped hard as the first sheets were taken off the press. The first two gospels were almost completed when the word came: 'Stop work!'

The thundering voice came from an army officer whose form filled the printing house doorway. Beyond him could be seen the glint of steel.

The powers from which Tyndale had escaped in England had been anything but asleep. The informer had been John Cochlaeus, a fanatic who had pledged himself to destroy anything that sounded like Reformation and to use any means to do so. He had tailed Tyndale and Roye from Wittenberg to Cologne, and infiltrated his way into Quentel's printing house and into the confidence of the printers. At work they talked little of the project in hand, but in the beer halls of Cologne in the evenings he found that tongues were loosened. Whether King Henry and Cardinal Wolsey wanted it or not, England would soon have a Reformation! He listened more attentively. And when the evening wore on and secret whisperings became a raucous hubbub he learned more. Two Englishmen – skilful in languages – a Testament in English! He pressed still closer. These Englishmen, who were they? But then mouths closed like vices. The fracas subsided; stares were hostile. The informer disappeared into the night.

But Cochlaeus had not given up. Pretending to be supervising another print job he again gained access to Quentel's printing house. He became acquainted with some of the master craftsmen and invited them to his lodgings. Beer was tippled and tongues were loosened. In Cochlaeus's own words, 'One of them in private conversation disclosed to me the secret by which England was to be won over to the party of Luther.' Bibles were already being printed in English. Costs were being met by wealthy London merchants who were to smuggle them into England and disperse them throughout the country before King and Cardinal could discover or prohibit it. Cochlaeus, having no further use for his guests, left them in their stupor and immediately contacted a city senator – Herman Rinck. Rinck was well known to the Emperor and the King of England. Distrusting Cochlaeus, however, Rinck planted another spy in the printing house, and from him received confirmation of the tale. Hence it was that, on the authority of the Senate of Cologne, the thundering voice of the Commander halted Quentel's printing works.

Flight

Tyndale and Roye immediately sensed danger. It was not only the printed sheets that the senator would wish to seize! Hurriedly, before the soldiers entered, Tyndale gathered the already printed ten sheets, and the pair left by a back entrance, making for the river. A fragment of Tyndale's New Testament printed at Quentel's (Matthew chapters 1-22) is in the British Museum.

For the second time Tyndale's hopes had been dashed and his plans blighted. The traitor within the gates had done his work. Then fresh plans had to be made, and made quickly! If their lives and manuscripts were to be preserved they needed to fly!

Meanwhile Rinck and Cochlaeus were composing letters to Henry VIII and Cardinal Wolsey. The 'wicked enterprise' of Tyndale and his friends was disclosed, and warning was given that English sea ports had to take precautions against the entrance of this 'pernicious merchandise'.

Tyndale and Roye waited in the warehouses at the Cologne quay-side for night to fall. When it did, they emerged from their lair and 'took ship' up the Rhine.

Smuggled to England

They must have travelled by water for some days. They would have passed Bonn, Coblenz and Mainz as the Rhine corridored through the steep defile of vine-clad, castle-capped hills.

Tyndale put ashore at Worms, a Protestant city. It was October. There he contacted a printer, Peter Schoeffer, and without loss of time his printing presses began rolling off English New Testaments.

Spalatinus, secretary to the Elector of Saxony, dined with Buschius, a well-known Renaissance scholar, and subsequently made this entry in his diary: 'Buschius told us that 6,000 copies of the New Testament have been printed in English. The work has been translated by an Englishman, staying there with two other Britons, who is so skilful in seven languages – Hebrew, Greek, Latin, Italian, Spanish, English and French – that whichever he speaks you would think it his native tongue.'[1]

Tyndale had been in Germany two years. By then 6,000 copies of the New Testament in English had been run off the presses at Worms. It was time for Monmouth and his merchant friends to play their part in shipping the Testaments concealed in their cargo into English ports. Hidden beneath bales of cloth, flour and other commodities, English New Testaments were being smuggled into England by the thousand.

Two copies of the Worms octavo survive: one at the Baptist College in Bristol, and the other at the library at St Paul's.

Despite Cardinal Wolsey's best efforts, a flourishing trade sprang up. In England 'distributing agencies' were already in place to be activated. The English Testaments from the Continent were soon finding eager buyers.

Burning the Bible

Tunstall and his fellow bishops were enraged. A fresh hue and cry for Tyndale and Roye was raised on the Continent. Movements had to be concealed. In August 1526, in England, a conclave of bishops resolved to 'burn all untrue translations of the Scriptures', and appointed Tunstall to strike at the centre of distribution – London.

Soon Tunstall, to the roar of the flames as they consumed the first English Testaments, was thundering out his famous sermons from St Paul's Cross. Few listened. But the flames continued avidly to devour.

While Tunstall was busy Bible-burning at St Paul's Cross, other bishops were buying up as many copies as they could lay their hands on. In one instance £70 was spent on one batch alone. This keen 'demand' from the Bible's enemies and their readiness to pay a good price stimulated the printers to fresh efforts, and soon Bibles were flooding the English coast in even greater quantities. The fact that, by then, Tyndale's translation had been pirated several times in Holland only served to increase the inundation.

In 1529 England signed a treaty in Antwerp. Tunstall was sent to represent the government. Knowing Antwerp to be an important centre of dispatch for Tyndale Testaments he made undercover enquiries among the merchants as to the sources of supply. In doing so he came across a London merchant called Augustin Packington. Packington seemed willing to do business, and Tunstall revealed his plan to buy up the Testaments. Packington was, it seemed, in an excellent position to buy up Tyndale Testaments and professed himself willing and able to fall in with the bishop's plans 'provided he had the wherewithal'. The bishop was jubilant. At last the heretical Testament would be removed from circulation. He would have been less jubilant had he known that Packington, a good friend of Tyndale's, was actually the kingpin in the plan by which Testaments were being smuggled into England.

He lost no time in acquainting Tyndale with his 'deal with the bishop'. 'I have gotten thee a merchant,' he said, 'which with ready money shall dispatch thee of all that thou hast!'

'Who is the merchant?' enquired Tyndale.

'The Bishop of London!'

The Bishop of London!

Tyndale was jubilant. His debts could be paid, and a revised edition of the New Testament launched. The bargain was struck.

When Tunstall, at a later date, complained to the sharp-witted Packington that the flow of Bibles into England had not ceased, Packington professed that he had done his part, but if the bishop would stem the flow he must buy up the printing presses. Tunstall realised that he had had the worst end of the bargain.

The truth was eventually ferreted out by England's new Chancellor, Sir Thomas More, from a man called George Constantine.

'My Lord,' said Constantine, 'will you that I tell you the truth? It is the Bishop of London that hath helpen us; for he bestoweth among us a great deal of money . . . and that is our only succour and comfort.'

On the run

While Tyndale's venture prospered, his enemies realised they had been defied and outwitted; so the campaign for his capture was speeded up.

Between 1527 and 1530 almost total mystery surrounds his whereabouts. By May 1527 Wolsey's agent in Antwerp, Hackett, was reporting that someone was translating the Old Testament into English. After the publication of the New Testament it is, in fact, likely that Tyndale remained for some time in Worms where he would have ready access to the Hebrew manuscripts. During this period he parted finally – and willingly – from his companion Roye. A renewed outbreak of persecution in England made it necessary to 'lie low'.

It was dangerous to be a Protestant, let alone a Protestant with known reformist views – *and* a Bible translator. In England, Sir Thomas More had lighted the fires of Smithfield, and many a Protestant martyr had been burned. Tyndale lived his life in constant awareness that any day, any moment, his whereabouts and identity would be discovered by an English or an Imperial agent, and that he would add more human fuel to the flames.[2]

Shipwrecked

During this period, too, he suffered another major setback. In Marburg he had continued his work of translating the first five books of the Old Testament. When it became apparent that enemy agents had tailed him to Marburg, he set out on a midnight flight to Antwerp. Alone and carrying only his books and copies, he set out on foot. He could travel only by night, and even then he avoided the main highways and skirted towns where possible.

He had not been in Antwerp long before it, too, became unsafe for him. This time he boarded a ship for Hamburg where he hoped to have his translation of the Pentateuch published. But, in the words of Bishop Foxe, 'Off the coast of Holland the ship was wrecked and he lost all his books, writings and copies, and so was compelled to begin anew.'

More than a year's work destroyed! He was saved. How, we do not know. But we *do* know that on his return to Antwerp he sailed again for Hamburg right away. He had faced difficulties before. This was no time for despair.

In Hamburg he met Miles Coverdale, who had not long arrived from Cambridge. Coverdale eventually was to complete his work for him. With Coverdale's assistance he began the process of retranslating the first five books of the Bible. The work was finally completed and published by John Hoochstraten in Antwerp on 17 January 1530.

In the months ahead he tackled a translation of the book of Jonah, very popular at that time. He also translated, but did not publish, the historical books of the Old Testament (Joshua to 2 Chronicles). In the course of the year following his publication of the Pentateuch he returned to Antwerp.

Safe passage to England?

Meanwhile changes were afoot in England. To achieve his divorce from Catherine of Aragon so that he could marry Anne Boleyn, Henry VIII had separated the English Church from the Church of Rome. In doing so he had made *himself* the head of the English Church. This turnaround in affairs in England also resulted in a turnaround in England's attitude towards Tyndale. Could his powerful pen be enlisted in the royal cause? Despite Tyndale's condemnation of the divorce, King Henry was persuaded by Thomas Cromwell to offer him safe conduct to England.[3]

The tricky assignment of making contact with Tyndale was given to a merchant called Stephen Vaughan. Repeated attempts were made to contact Tyndale, but without success. Where he was remained unknown.

Tyndale's friends told him about Vaughan's mission. After a while Vaughan was approached in the street and informed that a man was willing to meet him. To the messenger Vaughan replied, 'Who is your friend and where is he?'

'His name I know not, but if it be your pleasure to go where he is I will be glad thither to bring you,' replied the messenger.

Still no wiser, Vaughan was led through one of the worst parts of Antwerp – until he and his companion reached the edge of the city. Outside the city gates Vaughan's guide left. Looking around him, Vaughan could see no one until, when all was silent, a skinny form emerged from the shadows of the city wall.

' My name is Tyndale. . . .'

But he shook his head at the offer of safe passage. His work was not yet completed. Safe passage to England? The currents were still too changeable. The lean figure of Tyndale receded into the shadows. Vaughan was left with only a message for King Henry, and in that message the dearest hope of the man who had written it:

'If it would stand with the King's most gracious pleasure to grant only a bare text of the Scripture to be put forth among his people . . . be it of the translation of what person soever shall please His Majesty, I shall immediately make faithful promise never to write more, nor abide two days in these parts after the same; but immediately to repair unto his realm and humbly submit myself at the feet of His Royal Majesty, offering my body to suffer what pain or torture, yea, what death his grace will, so that this be obtained.'

Vaughan passed from the scene. Persuasion was again replaced by force, and the English ambassador to the Netherlands was issued with a directive to the effect, 'Get Tyndale, dead or alive!'

The closing of the net

But Tyndale had vanished. Somewhere he was engaged in revising his translation of the New Testament, but where no one knew. His revised editions were published in 1534 and 1535. The fires of Smithfield burned fiercely. In their fury Tyndale lost some of his best friends.

As 1534 faded, Tyndale was living in the house of an English merchant in Antwerp whose name was Thomas Poyntz. He was bringing his final revision of the New Testament to a close. Outside, the storm clouds were gathering. The emperor Charles V was determined to wipe out heresy in the Netherlands.

The end for Tyndale was to come about by a train of events initiated by Tunstall's successor as Bishop of London. His death was at the hands of the Imperial authorities.

The first dark shadows fell across Tyndale's path in the summer of 1535. The shadow was that of a man – Henry Phillips. A gambler, he had fallen on difficult times in London. In order to win back his fortune he had become a secret agent. His mission was to bring about the arrest of Tyndale.

Tyndale was completely fooled when Phillips first presented himself at the house of Thomas Poyntz. He invited him into the house and even secured him a night's lodging, showing him his translation. But Poyntz was not so easily fooled. Phillips soon learned that he would get no help from him.

Phillips' chance came when Poyntz went away on a six-week business trip. He invited Tyndale to dine. Tyndale accepted. When he went to collect his guest Phillips had the house surrounded with guards, with two on either side of the door to collar the unsuspecting Tyndale as soon as he emerged.

The corridor that led to the door of Poyntz's house at Antwerp was so narrow that the two men could not walk abreast, and Phillips pushed Tyndale on ahead. Being taller than Tyndale, Phillips, as one source has it, 'pointed with his finger over Tyndale's head down at him, that the officers on either side of the door might get the right man'. A few paces from the door, Tyndale saw the Spanish soldiers and stopped. But it was too late. The little man was carried bodily out of the door by Phillips.

Vilvorde

Later that day the drawbridge of the castle of Vilvorde closed behind him. The huge walls of Vilvorde made freedom seem a thousand miles away. Outside, the feeble hands of Poyntz defied them. Frantic attempts were made on Tyndale's behalf. But the evil genius of Henry Phillips again took a hand in the proceedings and Poyntz narrowly escaped arrest.

Tyndale's arrest had taken place in May 1535. The ensuing eighteen months were employed in writing his defence. But, in fact, the drawbridge had closed for ever. By October 1535 there was a chill in the air. The cells at Vilvorde became even more dark and dismal.

Towards the end of the year Tyndale wrote a letter to the authorities requesting 'a warmer cap'. He wrote, 'I suffer extremely from cold in the head, being afflicted with perpetual catarrh.' He asked too for a warmer coat, a patch for his leggings and, most of all, a Hebrew Bible and Hebrew grammar to pursue his translation. Whether he got them we do not know.

His requests were similar to those made in the letter that Paul smuggled to Timothy from his Roman prison. He, too, wanted his 'scrolls and parchments' – and a heavy overcoat to withstand the winter. Like Tyndale, Paul had looked back on a life of escapes, arrests and shipwreck.

When Tyndale next emerged into the light of day it was 6 October 1536. He was led to the centre of an enclosure at Vilvorde. Projecting through a small platform was a massive wooden cross. Round his throat was a loose-fitting rope, and around his neck and feet an iron chain secured him to the stake. On a signal from an officer the rope was tightened. When the flames began to lick his clothing Tyndale was already dead. On his lips was the immortal cry: '*Lord, open the King of England's eyes!*'

If Tyndale's death cry reflected his request to Henry VIII through Vaughan it was answered before it was uttered. Before the end of 1535, the previous year, in England the Bible Tyndale loved made its first semi-official appearance. Soon it bore the signature 'Henry Tudor'. The style of that Bible, as of many after it, was the style of Tyndale. Tyndale's memorial: The Bible in English.

References:

[1] Cited J. Isaacs, 'The Sixteenth Century English Versions', H. W. Robinson (ed, *The Bible its Ancient and English Versions*, page 153.

[2] For more detail on the relationship between William Tyndale and Sir Thomas More see Brian Moynahan, *If God Spare my Life: William Tyndale, the English Bible and Sir Thomas More – a Story of Martyrdom and Betrayal* (Little, Brown. 2002).

[3] A. G. Dickens, *The English Reformation*, page 111.

Towards King James

Before Tyndale was strangled and burned, his erstwhile enemy, Sir Thomas More, was beheaded. His conscience had not permitted him to follow his King through the policy of divorcing his Queen and separating from Rome. More and Tyndale, giants of their age, had spent years in argument, attacking and counter-attacking in pamphlet warfare. Now both were dead.[1]

More's replacement as Chancellor of England was Thomas Cromwell. Architect of the Tudor state, this subtle, political man also favoured reformation. The English Bible had made its semi-authorised appearance, having been brought together by Tyndale's disciple Miles Coverdale. Coverdale was under the direct patronage of Thomas Cromwell.

Coverdale's Bible

In December 1534 Thomas Cranmer, Archbishop of Canterbury, through the Convocation of Canterbury, petitioned the King to decree 'that the Holy Scripture shall be translated into the vulgar English tongue by certain upright and learned men to be named by the said most illustrious King'.

Coverdale's Bible made its appearance just twelve months after Cranmer's petition. It was the first complete English Bible and, while not strictly 'authorised', it was dedicated to Henry VIII. It was printed in Zurich.

Coverdale had produced his Bible in something of a hurry. Miles Coverdale (1488-1568) was an altogether more amenable character than Tyndale. In his preface he freely admitted his indebtedness to other translators (but not until the 1550 edition did he screw up the courage actually to name William Tyndale as one of them). But no one was under any illusions. Tyndale's style was too distinctive. Coverdale used all of Tyndale's work he could lay his hands on and, for the rest, he completed the translation himself from German and Latin Bibles.

When the second edition of Coverdale's Bible appeared in 1537 it was printed in England and actually licensed by the King. Over the next seventy-five years the work of revising and improving the Bible was almost continuous. 'Throughout, the work of Tyndale formed the foundation, and more than anyone else he established the rhythms and furnished much of the language which is familiar to us in our Authorised Version.'[2]

'Matthew's Bible'

As with the first edition of Coverdale's Bible in 1535, 'Matthew's Bible' of 1537 made its appearance as a result of the combined pressure of Thomas Cromwell and Thomas Cranmer. It received a royal licence.

Its popular name derived from the fact that the name Thomas Matthew appeared in its preface. It is likely that there was no such person and that John Rogers, who edited 'Matthew's Bible', used a false name to cover his tracks in case the King should once again change his mind about vernacular Bibles.[3] The alternative theory is that 'Thomas Matthew' was simply a pseudonym for Tyndale whose name was still anathema at court. Certainly Matthew's Bible was the one most closely associated with Tyndale. It silently incorporated Tyndale's unpublished version of the historical books of the Old Testament. Less wisely it incorporated, too, many of Tyndale's provocative prefaces and annotations.

In fact Rogers had brought together a composite. The Pentateuch, the historical books from Joshua to 2 Chronicles and the whole of the New Testament were Tyndale's; most of the remainder was Coverdale's work.

Neither of the two rival editions of 1537 was entirely satisfactory. Coverdale's Bible made good reading but the sections he had translated himself were notoriously distant from the original texts. 'Matthew's Bible', containing as it did Tyndale's provocative annotations, was too controversial.

The Great Bible

Towards the end of 1537 Thomas Cromwell gave Coverdale the task of 'cleaning up' and revising 'Matthew's Bible'. Thus began work on the Great Bible which was to make its appearance in 1539 and supersede the earlier Bibles.

To prepare the way for its arrival the clergy were charged on 5 September 1538: 'That ye shall provide, on this side of the Feast of All Saints next coming, one book of the whole Bible of the largest volume in English, and the same set up in some convenient place within the said church that ye have cure of, whereas your parishioners may most commodiously resort to the same and read it.'

Hence when the Great Bible appeared in 1539 it became the first formally authorised Bible for public use. Thomas Cranmer wrote the preface. But it was essentially Coverdale's revision of Matthew's Bible which was, in turn, John Rogers' revision of Tyndale's Bible.

It was an instant success. Vast crowds gathered around the six copies which were set up in St Paul's Cathedral. It ran through seven editions in two years.[4]

In the final years of his reign – 1540-1547 – Henry VIII reacted against moves towards Reformation. Thomas Cromwell was executed. But there was no dampening the English enthusiasm for the Bible. Some parishioners found the Great Bible so fascinating that they were reading aloud from it during divine service. The King had to issue a proclamation against this practice so that the priest could make himself heard!

Under Edward VI, editions of Tyndale's, Coverdale's, and the Great Bible poured from the presses. Mary's accession in 1553 put an end to that. Thomas Cranmer, Hugh Latimer and John Rogers paid the ultimate price for their enthusiasm for the reformed religion and the English Bible.

The Geneva Bible

Many English-Bible enthusiasts sought exile in Geneva during Mary's reign. There the work on Bible translation continued. The Geneva translators were happy with Tyndale's New Testament and the portion of the Old Testament translated by Tyndale. Hence their work was concentrated on that section of the Old Testament that Tyndale's arrest and imprisonment had prevented him from tackling. The Geneva New Testament was published in 1557 and the complete Geneva Bible in 1560. The greatest contribution of the Geneva Bible is an Old Testament entirely translated from Hebrew.

From a modern standpoint the most unfortunate thing about the Geneva Bible is the quantity of sectarian notes. They were unashamedly Calvinistic in doctrine and served as an irritant to, among others, the future James I. Nevertheless, for half a century the peoples of both England and Scotland read the Geneva Bible in preference to any other version and learned their theology from the appended notes.

Another novelty about the Geneva Bible was that it was divided into verses. The Hebrew Old Testament had first been divided into verses by Rabbi Nathan in 1448. The first Bible to contain the present verse divisions in both testaments had been Stephanus's Vulgate of 1555. The Geneva Bible simply followed these verse divisions.

The Geneva Bible became the household Bible of English-speaking Protestants in both Scotland and England. Since John Knox had been one of the Geneva exiles before leading the Scottish Reformation, it was natural that the Geneva Bible should be the version appointed to be read in Scottish churches.

Even when other Bibles had come along, including the King James version of 1611, the Geneva Bible held on to its devotees in both England and Scotland. When Oliver Cromwell's New Model Army went into battle in the English civil wars of the 1640s, each soldier took with him a copy of the Soldiers' Pocket Bible (the Geneva Bible under a new title).

The Geneva Bible was, by some, dismissed as the 'Breeches

Bible'. The Geneva translators followed the Wycliffite versions in making Genesis 3:7 read that Adam and Eve sewed fig leaves together and made themselves 'breeches'.

The Bishops' Bible

By the time of Thomas Cromwell's execution in 1540, a project had been afoot to prepare a vernacular Bible under the direct supervision of the English bishops. It had come to nothing. In 1561 Elizabeth I's Archbishop of Canterbury, Matthew Parker, revived the idea. He submitted to the bishops a proposal that they should revise the Great Bible.

A scholar of considerable standing, Parker was eminently qualified to act as editor-in-chief. The actual work of translation, however, was 'subcontracted out' to a number of scholars, some of whom were already bishops and some of whom were to become bishops.

The 'Bishops' Bible' was completed in seven years and copies were sent to the Queen on 22 September 1568. The Convocation of Canterbury ordered that it should be used in all cathedrals and churches as far as possible.

King James

James I, who acceded in 1603, had some pretensions to be a Bible scholar. As King James VI of Scotland he had already written a *Paraphrase upon the Revelation of St John* and had translated the Psalms into metre.[5]

But James was prejudiced against the Geneva version. Since it was the first Bible ever published in Scotland (1579), given that it had been dedicated to him, and having regard to the fact that it was the version from which he quoted in his own writings, we find his prejudice rather surprising. Almost certainly it was purely on the grounds that its margins were loaded with sectarian commentary.

In January 1604, not long after the King's accession, the Hampton Court Conference was convened. Dr John Reynolds, president of Corpus Christi College, Oxford, the leader of the Puritan wing of the Church of England, proposed that there be a new translation of the Bible.

The resolution passed was 'that a translation be made of the whole Bible, as consonant as can be to the original Hebrew and Greek; and this to be set out and printed, without any marginal notes, and only to be used in all churches of England in time of divine service'.

The King was enthusiastic. However, the clause regarding marginal notes was doubtless included on his insistence. 'I wish some special pains were taken for an uniform translation,' he said, 'which should be done by the best-learned men in both universities, then reviewed by the bishops, presented to the Privy Council, lastly ratified by royal authority to be read in the whole church and none other.'

The King himself took a leading part in organising the work of translation. He undertook no translation himself. Six panels of translators (forty-seven men in all) had the work divided among them. Three panels were responsible for the Old Testament, two for the New, and one for the Apocrypha. Two of the panels met at Oxford, two at Cambridge, and two at Westminster. When the panels had completed their work, the draft translation was reviewed by a smaller group of twelve men, two from each panel, before the work was sent to the printer.

The payments made to the translators were tiny, but James promised them ecclesiastical preferment, and was as good as his word.

The King had drawn up the ground rules for the translators himself. The Bishops' Bible was to serve as the basis for the new translation. Marginal notes were to be used only to explain Hebrew and Greek words, to draw attention to parallel passages and to make the sense plainer. Words necessary to complete the sense of the text were to be printed in italics. Existing chapter and verse divisions were to be retained.

The Authorised Version made its appearance in 1611 and went through three editions within the year. There is a sense in which it represented Tyndale's dream fulfilled. Professor J. Isaacs has written: 'Tyndale's honesty, sincerity and scrupulous integrity, his simple directness, his magical simplicity of phrase, his modest music, has given an authority to his wording that has imposed itself on all later versions. With all the tinkering to which the New Testament has been subject, Tyndale's version is still the basis in phrasing, rendering, vocabulary and rhythm, and often in music as well. Nine tenths of the Authorised New Testament is still Tyndale, and the best is still his.'[6]

References:

[1] On the relationship between Tyndale and More see Brian Moynahan, *If God Spare My Life: William Tyndale, The English Bible and Sir Thomas More — a Story of Martyrdom and Betrayal* (Little, Brown. 2002).

[2] Sir Frederic Kenyon, *The Story of the Bible*, page 49.

[3] B. F. Westcott, *A General View of the History of the English Bible* (third edition), pages 67, 68.

[4] A. G. Dickens, *The English Reformation*, page 190.

[5] J. Isaacs, 'The Authorised Version and After', H. W. Robinson (ed), *The Bible in its Ancient and English Versions*, page 197.

[6] J. Isaacs, *op cit*, pages 160, 204, 205.

A moving target

The King James Bible

'The King James Bible may indeed be esteemed as an excellent translation . . . by the standards of 1611 and beyond. Yet translations eventually require revision, not necessarily because they are defective, but because the language into which they're translated itself changes over time. Translation involves aiming at a moving target, which has accelerated over the centuries. . . .'[1]

The King James Bible was attacked from all quarters as soon as it appeared.

Some preferred the Bishops' Bible. Many more preferred the Geneva Bible. There was a mood of intolerance.

The translators were not taken by surprise.

Up front the early editions of the King James Bible had a preface entitled 'The Translators to the Reader'. That preface was a humble appeal on the part of the translators to give the new version a fair chance. Their work had, said the translators, been 'welcomed with suspicion instead of love'.

The translators of 'the King James' were very generous in their praise of previous translations.

Interesting.

In the last half century the tables have been turned. The supporters of the King James Bible have been attacking more modern versions. It is always a paradox to hear those who love and defend the King James Version oppose other translations. They are acting against the spirit of those who produced the Bible they are defending.

'Translation involves aiming at a moving target, which has accelerated over the centuries. English is developing more quickly today than at any time in its previous history. Some words have ceased to be used; others have changed their meanings. When a translation itself requires translation, it has ceased to serve its original purpose.'[1]

The King James Bible translators were committed to translating God's Word *into living English*. In short, to make the Word *accessible* to ordinary readers. It was also in the interests of accessibility that they incorporated the chapter and verse divisions of earlier versions and that they punctuated the text so heavily.

'The prose of the King James Bible had the power to move and convert, and exercised a powerful hold over the mental world of generations of English-speaking people,' writes a recent authority. The power and influence of that Bible 'will not end, until either history is brought to a close or English ceases to be a living language.'[2] Nevertheless, the 'beautiful', powerful English of the KJV was never *spoken* English – at any time. To that extent it was always somewhat 'artificial'.

In the eighteenth century John Wesley was acutely aware of the need, once again, to make the Word accessible to a new generation; the high-flown English of the KJV, together with massive changes in the use of the language over the preceding century, meant that it was largely incomprehensible to the working classes to which the industrial revolution had given rise. Nevertheless, the literary influence of the KJV was never greater than in the eighteenth and nineteenth centuries.

Catholic versions

Before the publication of the KJV, an English Bible had been produced for Roman Catholic readers. Other Catholic Bibles were produced in the twentieth century.

The Council of Trent in 1546 laid down that the 'ancient and Vulgate version, which is approved by its long use in so many centuries in the Church itself, be held as authentic in public lectures, disputations, sermons and expository discourses. . . .' Hence both the 'Douai Bible' of 1578 and the Ronald Knox version of the twentieth century followed the Wycliffite tradition (as opposed to the Tyndale tradition) of the English Bible.

Much of the credit for the Douai version must go to William Allan, a fellow at an Oxford college who had refused to acquiesce in the Elizabethan religious settlement and fled to France to become the founder of an English college at Douai. By the mid-eighteenth century the Douai version was largely unintelligible to most English-speaking Catholics. Therefore in 1749 Bishop Richard Challoner undertook a major revision. That, in turn, incorporated revisions undertaken in the previous century by Gregory Martin.

King James: the need for revision

At the beginning of the twentieth century, Wesley's eighteenth-century concerns notwithstanding, the King James Version was still the one most commonly used in the English-speaking world. The demands for revision, heard since the eighteenth century, were largely muted among Protestant Christians until well into the twentieth century.

The demands for revision were twofold: 1. The desire for a Bible in the 'English of the common man' to whom the lofty prose of the KJV was unintelligible. 2. The desire for greater textual accuracy.

What really fuelled demands for a revision of the KJV was the discovery of no fewer than 4,500 manuscripts of the Greek New Testament – in whole or in part – most of which dated from a period much nearer to the apostles than the manuscripts from which Tyndale and subsequent translators had worked. Most notable of all, of course, was the discovery of the *Codex Sinaiticus*. 'It became increasingly clear that the Authorised Version required to be revised in order to be brought into closer conformity with the Greek text of the New Testament, as established by more intensive textual study on the basis of more reliable evidence than had been accessible in 1611.'[3]

Modern authorities have estimated that no fewer than 150,000 variants were discovered between the different Greek manuscripts available. They are emphatic, however, that none of them alters either the picture of God which emerges from Scripture or any fundamental Christian doctrine. Nevertheless, it will be understood that before that was clearly grasped – in the last two decades of the nineteenth century – there was an express desire on the part of many scholars to find out how a translation of the earliest manuscripts would change their understanding of Scripture.

As the man in the pew became aware that the scholars were undertaking detailed study of the most ancient Greek manuscripts with a view to a possible revised English Bible, he began to worry.

In fact, conscientious scholars, each one keeping a close eye on the others' work, were burning midnight oil in Europe and in the United States of America. Each newly discovered ancient manuscript was pored over as it was discovered. Whole lifetimes were spent in the pursuit of textual accuracy. Translators were not in any way surprised to find variations among the manuscripts. They could well imagine the difficulties involved in copying out the original Hebrew, Aramaic and Greek. When the copyists were doing their work in the early Christian centuries, chapters and verses had not been invented; there were no separations between the words (and, therefore, there was the possibility of a number of different ways of reading a particular collection of words); there was no punctuation; in Hebrew there were no vowels!

What the scholars *were* surprised to discover was the minimal importance of the variations as they came to light. The fact was that, while the wording frequently had to be altered, the understanding had hardly ever changed.[4]

What the discovery of the variations *did* provide, however, was an unassailable case for a revision of the King James Bible. Henry Alford, dean of Canterbury, began to argue in that way as early as 1869. A Royal Commission was established to revise the Authorised Version. In 1870, by the action of the Convocation of Canterbury, work was begun which would eventually lead to the publication of the Revised Version. Members of the Church of Scotland and the English and Scottish free churches were represented on the translation committees. As the revision proceeded, American scholars were also involved.

The New Testament section of the Revised Version was published in May 1881 and the Old Testament in May 1885. In 1901 the American scholars produced their own American Standard Version.

Catholic versions

Ronald Knox was not the only Roman Catholic involved in the production of a modern Bible. Twenty-eight Roman Catholic scholars produced *The Jerusalem Bible* in 1966. As with previous translations they also translated the fourteen books of the Apocrypha. Since Luther, 'Protestant' Bibles had placed the apocryphal books between the two Testaments. Roman Catholic versions, including the Jerusalem Bible, dispersed them through the Old Testament. Unlike previous Roman Catholic versions, however, *The Jerusalem Bible* was a translation from the original languages, not from Jerome's Vulgate. The quality of the work of the translators of *The Jerusalem Bible* brought many accolades from Protestant and Jewish scholars.

The New American Bible and *The New Jerusalem Bible*, subsequent Catholic translations, have also received many accolades from non-Catholics.

Versions in modern English

The pedantic accuracy and precision with which those who produced the Revised Version did their work made it an admirable version for the student. The variations found in the *Codex Sinaiticus* and the *Codex Vaticanus* were incorporated either into the text of the Revised Version or into the footnotes.

But there was still a problem: the old-fashioned language.

A. M. Hunter, writing in 1951, expressed the feeling of many scholars since the beginning of the century:

'Since the famous forty-seven did their work in 1611, nearly three-and-a-half centuries have passed. In that time our speech has so changed that the Authorised Version, for all the glories of its language, has grown more and more of a foreign tongue. The common man does not speak or properly understand the great accents of his Elizabethan ancestors. Were the Christian teacher or preacher concerned only with literary appreciation he might rest content with the Authorised Version, but his task, being what it is – to preach and teach the word of God to a generation that is almost biblically illiterate and slowly lapsing into paganism – he demands, and rightly demands, a version of the New Testament that will clothe the word of the Gospel in the vesture of our common speech. . . .'[5]

Many scholars express the argument this way. The Greek in which the New Testament was written was not classical Greek. It was the *koine*, street language Greek. If the people of Paul's day could read the Scriptures in their everyday language, why should not the English-speaking people have the same privilege?

With modern speech and textual accuracy in mind, Dr Richard Weymouth, a fellow of University College, London, having published a Greek New Testament, published *The New Testament in Modern Speech* in 1903. Sadly, Weymouth's New Testament did not live up to the title he gave it. It contained a great deal of 'translators' English', awkward, 'wooden' self-expression, together with many words and phrases long since dropped from ordinary speech.

Arguably, the breakthrough was made by the brilliant Scottish scholar Dr James Moffatt. Moffatt published his New Testament in 1913, his Old Testament in 1924, and his complete one-volume Bible, *A New Translation of the Bible*, in 1928.

Moffatt's version was the one that really shocked the religious establishment. Though an academic, he had a considerable grasp of secular language and was not afraid to use it in place of the pious language readers expected to find in their Bibles.

But Moffatt was first a scholar. Unlike Weymouth, Moffatt was fluent in Hebrew as well as Greek. Both languages came across in free and vigorous English.

In 1927 Moffatt's American counterpart, Dr Edgar Goodspeed, produced *The Complete Bible: An American Translation*. His rationalisation for 'an American translation' was that even contemporary English 'familiar in England or Scotland' was 'strange in American ears'.

Recent translations

Before the outbreak of World War II the idea was floated that committees of British, American and Canadian scholars should work together on a new revision – in the light of recent manuscript discoveries and of changes in the use of English – of the Revised Version of 1885 and the *American Standard Version* of 1901. The war intervened, and the American and Canadian committees went to work on their own. The resultant *Revised Standard Version* was published in 1952. As with Goodspeed, the *Revised Standard Version* received as warm a welcome in Britain as it did in Canada and the United States.

When the war ended there was a different mood abroad in Britain. The mood affected the leadership of the Church of England, the Church of Scotland and the major Nonconformist denominations. The mood was against another mere revision of the Authorised Version and in favour of a completely new translation in modern speech.

It is likely that this mood had been sparked off in the war years by Dr J. B. Phillips. Pastor of a parish which frequently experienced heavy night-time bombardment from the Luftwaffe, Phillips found that Christianity acquired a new relevance among his parishioners. His ideal was to infuse the youth of his congregation with the same sense of relevance. He set about doing this by introducing them to the letters of Paul. He believed that the constant threat of persecution under which the early churches laboured was not unlike the constant threat of annihilation under which the wartime Londoners lived. After youth club activities Phillips would read a few verses from Paul's letters, 'After all, I thought to myself, much of this was written by one Christian in difficulty to other Christians in difficulty, and surely these young people will find them appropriate to their situation.' But Phillips was disappointed, 'I was met by polite but complete lack of comprehension. The youngsters, who were by no means unintelligent, simply did not understand Bible language.'[6]

Phillips had been a brilliant scholar at Cambridge and had an excellent grasp of Greek. Throughout his ministry he had had a 'passion for making truth comprehensible'. He had also developed an enviable ability to communicate with all age and social groups in a form of English that was both intelligible and compelling. He was familiar with the other modern translations undertaken in the twentieth century and quietly deplored the stuffy, 'translators' English' in which they were written.

In his busy wartime schedule Dr Phillips set aside one morning each week for translating Paul's letters. When he had completed the letter to the Colossians he sent a copy to C. S. Lewis of Magdalen College, Oxford. He received his reply on 3 August 1943. Lewis wrote: 'Thank you a hundred times. I thought I knew Colossians pretty well, but your paraphrase made it far more significant – it was like seeing a familiar picture after it's been cleaned.' Lewis encouraged Phillips to complete all of Paul's letters and to publish them under the title of *Letters to Young Churches*.

As he worked on his translation, Phillips tried it out on his youth groups and found an instant and positive response. *Letters to Young Churches* was finally published in 1947 with a preface written by C. S. Lewis. It was an immediate success. Within a short time J. B. Phillips was being interviewed on both radio and television. In no time his fame had spread across the Atlantic. In 1952 he published *The Gospels in Modern English*.

There can be little doubt that it was the early success of J. B. Phillips that ignited the enthusiasm in the established churches of England and Scotland to produce a completely new translation of the English Bible. The general assembly of the Church of Scotland adopted the motion in 1946. They then approached the Church of England and the principal free churches, and gradually won the approval of each. The inevitable joint committee was established in 1947. Dr C. H. Dodd was appointed convenor for the New Testament panel. Dodd tells us that each book, or part of a book, was at first entrusted to an individual translator, before the committee got to work on it.

What resulted was the *New English Bible*. The New Testament appeared in 1961 and the complete Bible – one edition included the Apocrypha – appeared in 1970.

Of the 'hundreds of one-man versions',[7] J. B. Phillips' without question came nearest to the needs of the common man. In 1972 he published a revised edition of *The New Testament in Modern English* in which he incorporated more than 2,000 changes.

For some, however, the modern versions which emerged out of America in the 1970s and 1980s eclipsed Phillips'. Certainly the popular paraphrase, *The Living Bible*, first published in 1971, rivals Phillips' for readability. That was purely and simply the paraphrase of Dr John Taylor. However, a committee of scholars combined its accessibility with great accuracy in the *New Living Translation* that appeared in 1996.

The aim of Phillips to avoid theological terms and pious phraseology was taken over by the translators of the *Good News Bible*, another version (translation) that rivals Phillips' for readability. It was first published – in 1976 – by the American Bible Society.

The *New International Version*, translated by a group of conservative, evangelical scholars and published by the New York Bible Society, seeks to combine readability with textual accuracy – and succeeds. First published in 1977, it was beginning to appear as a kind of 'new authorised version' among evangelical Nonconformists by the end of the twentieth century.

For a time it seemed that for scholars, preachers and ordinary readers, *The Revised English Bible* (first published in 1989 by Oxford and Cambridge) combined the best of all worlds. It had begun as a revision of the *New English Bible* but, as the translators had recourse to the Hebrew and Greek manuscripts and had involved contemporary writers in their work, it had emerged as a totally new translation.

When the *New Revised Standard Version* (a revision of the RSV) was published in 1989, that, too, was given plaudits for its accuracy. It also used gender-inclusive language.

When the updated edition of the *New American Standard Bible* appeared in 1995, it was clear that priority had been given to accuracy over fluidity of language. Nevertheless it has, and will retain, a following on both sides of the Atlantic Ocean.

The reverence for the King James Bible is still very much alive, especially among fundamentalist Christians. In 1982 a 'Revised

Authorised Version' of the King James Bible – retaining the grandeur of its language but removing its more obvious archaisms – was published in the United States.

Many are confused by the sheer number of different translations now available and ask the question, 'Which version is best?' The response to that question has to be, 'Best – for what?'

The only way to find out which version is best for you is to visit a library or bookshop, take the various versions off the shelves – and sample them.

Do any of the versions contain theological bias? After a lifetime of research and comparison, immersed in the Greek in which the New Testament was written, Dr A. Graham Maxwell, a retired professor from Loma Linda University, has said: 'I've gone through every version looking for signs of theological bias, and have found it so rare as to be conspicuous.' The Bible translators, insists Maxwell, have been very honest men; all versions come ultimately from the same Hebrew, Aramaic and Greek. 'And that's where the great safety lies. The scholars are constantly watching one another.'

As Alister McGrath has written, however: 'Translation involves aiming at a moving target, which has accelerated over the centuries. English is developing more quickly today than at any time in its previous history.' That being the case there are still those who catch Tyndale's vision to target the masses with popular, vernacular versions. Biblical languages expert Eugene H. Peterson began publishing *The Message* paraphrase in 1993. By 2002 he was able to publish the whole Bible in a contemporary paraphrase. Peterson has a real flair for current English and his paraphrase has provided the current generation with a Bible they can read, and an older generation with brand-new spiritual insights.

Rob Lacey caught the J. B. Phillips vision to make the Bible comprehensible to street youth in particular. When Lacey first published *The Street Bible* in 2003 (Zondervan), many wondered whether it would be, in fact, in the language of the streets. They were amazed at Lacey's MTV-style dialogue and consistent use of contemporary urban language. Here is how *The Street Bible* renders John 11:25-26:

*Jesus says, 'I'm the Death of Death. I'm Life with a capital "L".
Invest all you've got in me and you'll live, and that includes dead
people. You put it all on the line for me and you'll never die.'*
Gifted, creative people are still aiming at that moving target!

References:
[1] Alister McGrath, *In the Beginning: the Story of the King James Bible* (Hodder and
Stoughton. 2001), page 308-309.
[2] Ibid, pages 303, 310.
[3] F. F. Bruce, *The English Bible*, page 128.
[4] The most important variants are dealt with above in the chapter entitled, 'The Find of a
Lifetime'.
[5] A. M. Hunter, *Interpreting the New Testament 1900-1950*.
[6] J. B. Phillips, *The Price of Success: An Autobiography*, pages 99, 100.
[7] Pearl Sjolander, *Some Aspects of Style in Twentieth-century English Bible Translation*, page 9.

4

Archaeology and the *Bible*

Wanted!
A key to the ancient world

The lands of the Middle and Near East had been magnets for pilgrims from the third century.

In the millennia before Christ, civilisations had left their stories in stone. But they were unread and, it was assumed, unreadable.

Nevertheless, in the eighteenth century, driven by demand from the West for the treasures of long-dead civilisations in the East, some adventurers began to rummage – with an eye on the cash prize.

Among the exciting 'discoveries' they stumbled upon were the cities of Baalbek, Palmyra and Petra. In Egypt they had the most rewarding time. However, their fantastic accounts of pyramids and temples and painted tombs were no more than travellers' tales.

Wanted. A key to unlock the door to the ancient world: Egyptian picture language (hieroglyphics).

Most doubted that such a key existed.

Meanwhile Enlightenment scholars were debunking the Bible. Their argument went something like this:

As history, the Old Testament was totally unreliable. Abraham and his family had not begun the patriarchal line; they had lived at the time of the kings of Israel – or even later. The so-called 'laws of Moses' had nothing whatever to do with Moses, but had been written by priests at the time of the Exile. Indeed, Moses would probably have been unable to write. As for the nation of the Hittites which loomed so large in Old Testament narratives, that was a mythical race; there was consensus on that point. The

Assyrian and Babylonian kings whose names and doings pep-
pered the Old Testament may be discounted, the odd one might
have existed, but most were the invention of the ever-fecund
Hebrew imagination.

The 'experts' were guilty of bad timing as well as misinforma-
tion. No sooner had they debunked the Bible to their mutual
satisfaction than the first of the elusive keys was discovered.

The Rosetta Stone

The Rosetta Stone was the key to the secrets of ancient Egypt
which, in turn, shed considerable light on the history of other
nations — and on the Bible narrative.

When Napoleon invaded Egypt in 1798 he took with him 175
French scholars. He was acutely aware of Egypt as a treasure-
house of the past. Before the Battle of the Pyramids, he told his
commanders: 'Forty centuries look down upon you!'

Napoleon's scholars made maps and went in search of treasures
to be transported back to France. Near Rosetta on the Nile a
fascinating stone was found. Much later it was discovered to
contain the record of a decree of King Ptolemy V in three languages: hieroglyphs (top); demotic script (middle); and Greek
(bottom).

The ships chartered by Napoleon's scholars, loaded with
ancient artefacts including the Rosetta Stone, were intercepted by
the British fleet before they reached France. Most of the booty
found its way to the British Museum where it still is.

Recognising the first language of the stone to be hieroglyphs
and very much aware that the inscription on the tombs and
temples of Egypt were written in hieroglyphs, the French scholars
had taken a plaster cast of the Rosetta Stone. Hence, in the years
after the Egyptian campaign, scholars in both London and Paris
were studying the three languages of the Rosetta Stone.

Reading the Greek was easy. Once it was established that the
identical decree was being given in all three languages, the
demotic script was also deciphered. The really difficult part, however, was making sense of the hieroglyphic script.

Jean-Francois Champollion takes the principal credit for

deciphering Egyptian hieroglyphics. Having pored over many hieroglyphic inscriptions in different parts of Egypt, he became fascinated by the first language on the Rosetta Stone. Making sense of it became an obsession with him. In 1822 he realised something of vital importance: the hieroglyphs were not simply symbols or letters – they represented sounds, and whole words. It was thus that he broke the most difficult of the scripts and, in doing so, unlocked the history of a nation that cut a swathe right across the Old Testament.

The ancient monuments of Egypt were covered with hieroglyphics which had remained dumb for 2,000 years. They were about to speak.

As exponents of the new-born science of archaeology converged on Egypt to read the record of its past, they were well aware that archaeology could not 'prove' or 'disprove' God, or whether God spoke through Moses or Isaiah or any of the other Bible prophets. However, they also knew that if they could find evidence of the existence of particular individuals or nations whose existence had been denied by the 'experts', and if they could ascertain that the chronology of the Bible narrative – denied by 'experts' – was in fact accurate, they were in a position to give the lie to the 'debunking' school of thought. Or, at least, to introduce a little humility into some of its pronouncements.

The Behistun Rock

The understanding of Egyptian hieroglyphs represented just one key to unlock the ancient world.

Another form of writing used in most parts of the Middle East was called *cuneiform*.

Cuneiform means 'wedge-shaped'. It was a name invented for a certain type of writing by French and English archaeologists and derives from the Latin. Cuneiform was used widely in the Eastern world for over 3,000 years.

It was developed by the original Sumerian inhabitants of Babylonia. It was commonplace at the beginning of the patriarchal period. Abraham's departure from Ur is believed to have taken place about the time of Hammurabi (*circa* 1850BC). One thousand years before Hammurabi chiselled his code of laws on a slab of stone, the Sumerians had begun to use cuneiform.

In the early years of archaeological excavation, clay tablets containing cuneiform script were being found throughout the Middle East. They fascinated the scholars. It was clear to them that cuneiform had developed out of the same kind of pictorial script as hieroglyphs. In Babylonia, however, the almost complete absence of stone had compelled the scribe to make use of clay. At first, attempts had been made to draw pictures upon the clay. Soon, however, the scribe had found it more convenient just to press the edge of his square-ended stick or stylus into the soft clay and so to build up his characters, not by outline but by a series of triangular or wedge-shaped characters.

Cuneiform was found in Egypt, but it is clear that it did not displace hieroglyphs. Abraham would have encountered it in Ur, and might have encountered it in Egypt. It would have accompanied him all along the trade route north-west of Syria, then south-west through Canaan. Centuries later a man like Moses 'learned in all the wisdom of the Egyptians' would have been able to read and reproduce both hieroglyphs and cuneiform. The Tell el Amarna Tablets, written close to the Mosaic era, indicate that even Canaanite-speaking people could produce cuneiform. Hence it is clear that throughout the patriarchal period Bible characters are likely to have been literate. In the light of recent research, far from questioning the ability of Moses to write, we may even conjecture that he might have progressed beyond clumsy syllabic scripts to an alphabetical style of writing, not dissimilar to the Hebrew of a later age.

Making sense of the different variations in cuneiform script was the second key that unlocked the history of the ancient world.

The story of how cuneiform was finally 'cracked' by the scholars is tied up with the Behistun Rock.

For centuries travellers between Tehran and Baghdad had had to pass by the massive rock face at Behistun. They had looked up and seen, 300 feet above road level, a detailed carving. A number of men figured in the carving, and a large area surrounding it had been rendered smooth.

Over the years climbers had ventured up to take a closer look. They had noticed marks cut into the smooth stone. Drawings were made of the marks and scholars puzzled over the drawings – but made no sense of them.

Carsten Niebuhr, an expert in Arabic, was perhaps the first to make an attempt to decipher what was clearly writing of some sort. He saw that there were three different kinds of scripts.

George Grotefend, a German schoolmaster, was the next to attempt to decipher the script on the Behistun Rock. He actually identified the names of Darius and Xerxes. But it was to take a great many more years before the Behistun inscriptions were the means of deciphering Persian cuneiform. It was to be the achievement of Englishman Henry Rawlinson.

In 1836 Rawlinson began work on the Behistun texts. Working in intense heat at the top of a ladder cannot have made things easy. At times he found himself perched on a ledge only eighteen inches wide. In 1837 he completed his translation of 200 lines. From his transcription, Persian cuneiform had been deciphered within ten years.

Rawlinson had identified other types of cuneiform writing on the cliff face at Behistun. One of them incorporated over a hundred signs, too many to be an alphabet. Only long years of study and assistance from experts employed by the Royal Asiatic Society, enabled him to decipher Susian or Elamite cuneiform. That had been done by 1855.

But, as with the Rosetta Stone, there were actually *three* languages on the Behistun Rock. Rawlinson turned his attention to the third. He had the indispensable help of an Anglican clergyman, Edward Hincks, and a Kurdish boy who risked life and limb on a daily basis to take impressions from inaccessible parts of the rock face. The language turned out to be Assyrian or Babylonian cuneiform. It was identified and deciphered in 1857.

As a key to the past, the third language of Behistun was more important than the rest. For 2,500 years the records of Assyria and Babylonia had been silent. Thanks to Rawlinson and his helpers, they could speak.

The Old Testament contained a tremendous amount of detailed information about both Assyria and Babylonia. When Babylonian cuneiform had been deciphered, archaeologists were in a position to discover whether it was fact or fiction.

Treasure tells

The third key to unlock the world of the Bible was the Middle Eastern *tells*.

A tell is a flat-topped mound, without interest to the uninformed.

It is fortunate for modern archaeology that tells *were* without interest for many centuries. A virgin tell is a city with its history intact, waiting to be read by the archaeologist and his team. Its history may stretch back three, four, even five thousand years.

A tell is invariably found near a water source. In the mists of the past a collection of families would take a decision to build a community, often in a defensible position. Around their community or settlement they would build ramparts of mud or brick.

With the passage of centuries their town would be destroyed by enemies. Families would then rebuild on the same site (for the same reasons that the settlement was established there in the first place), building over the ruins of the first settlement. Depending upon the scale of destruction, there might be long periods in which the settlement might be left abandoned. In the event, the rain, driven by the prevailing west wind, would wash the debris of house walls and roofs off the site, until further erosion was checked by the arrival of another collection of families and the rebuilding of fortifications and dwellings.

As successive occupations would follow one upon another, a tell would gradually develop. Each occupation would be marked by its own stratum, like the layers of a cake. With each new settlement the area of development would decrease slightly and the town be built farther from ground level. Eventually the tell would reach a considerable height. For example, the tell of Beth-Shan is seventy feet high.

The number of strata varies from one tell to another. The area of a tell varies from between 2.5 acres to 13 acres. The tell of Hazor north of Galilee is 100 acres.

Each stratum will contain not just masonry but pottery of various kinds. The profusion of pottery in Middle Eastern tells enabled archaeologists to date each stratum even prior to the use of carbon-14 dating. Amulets were found frequently. A *stele* (tablet) covered with hieroglyphs or a cylinder-seal or a cuneiform tablet was a real find.

At first archaeologists simply worked 'downwards'. They began with the topmost stratum, clearing away the loose debris until walls, rooms and artefacts emerged. When a stratum was finished with, the walls were simply removed – and the next tratum tackled. This 'working downwards' method was known to archaeologists as the Reisner-Fisher technique.

In 1952-58 Dame Kathleen Kenyon applied Sir Mortimer Wheeler's trench method on Jericho. The results were so brilliant that trenching has become standard practice. Before excavation a trench is dug through *all* the layers of the mound. That is now known as the Wheeler-Kenyon technique. It supplemented but did not displace the Reisner-Fisher technique. The careful use of test trenches helps to determine exact stratification before digging an area, and is followed by additional test trenches at right-angles to walls as they are cleared.

When an excavation is completed the material is prepared for publication; everything meticulously recorded, drawn and photographed.

The discovery of the nature of the tell and the development of the various techniques to interpret its contents has provided a vast amount of information about the cities mentioned in Bible times. Babylon, Ninevah, Susa, Ur, Jericho, Megiddo, Samaria and Hazor are just a few of the Bible cities which, having been silent for centuries, have yielded their secrets to the archaeologist's spade. Not only have they provided valuable background colour to life in Old Testament times, but their cuneiform-covered *steles* have authenticated matters of detail.

The doors to the ancient world have been unlocked. We can peer back down the ages – watch the armies of Caesar,

Alexander, Cyrus and Sennacherib. In the distance we can see patriarchs and pharaohs, prophets and kings. Then, as the evidence of the spade confirms the book time after time, we experience exhilaration, and more. Much more. For the Bible is far more than the most detailed, accurate, ancient-history book.

The great empires of the East

By 1865 the door to the World of the Bible was open.

The ancient languages had been deciphered. The inscriptions were yielding their mysteries.

When the realisation – at the same time – that a tell represented accumulations of layers of occupation, the great age of biblical archaeology was under starter's orders.

In Britain, France, Germany and the United States funds were made available to finance the work of this new breed of scientist: the archaeologist.

Soon archaeological finds were front-page news in Western newspapers.

The names of Egyptian pharaohs, dead for three-and-a-half millennia, became household words. Discussion began: Who was the pharaoh who enslaved the Israelites? Who was the pharaoh at the time of the Exodus? *When* was the Exodus?

Images of the Assyrian tyrants mentioned in Scripture were found carved on their palace walls, with their armies and their miserable captives.

The great kings of Persia began to speak through their writings.

As the tells of Palestine and Iraq were excavated, evidence was found that corroborated and added colour to the Bible record.

The history books of the Old Testament came alive!

Sir Henry Layard, Hormuz Rassam and Paul Emile Botta discovered the long-forgotten cities of Nineveh and Babylon.

Babylon: city of gold

For centuries Babylon had been the key metropolis of Mesopotamia – the land between the Tigris and Euphrates rivers, now called Iraq. It flourished for nearly 2,000 years until its capture by Alexander the Great in 331BC. Famous kings like Hammurabi and Nebuchadnezzar presided over the days of its glory. The Greeks remembered it as containing *two* of the seven wonders of the ancient world.

At the height of Babylon's splendour, the Hebrew prophet Isaiah wrote: 'Babylon, the jewel of kingdoms, the glory of the Babylonians' pride, will be overthrown by God.' (Isaiah 13:19, NIV.)

In 1807 Claudius Rich – who could read Arabic, Syriac, Hebrew and Persian – became the East India Company's representative in Baghdad. In 1811, accompanied by his teenage bride, he made his first excursion to Babylon. He set men to dig for inscribed tablets, seals and sculpted walls. His report and sketches, published as *Memoirs of the Ruins of Babylon*, described Babylon along the lines Isaiah had prophesied. 'No Arab will pitch his tent there, no shepherd will rest his flocks there. But desert creatures will lie there, jackals will fill her houses. . . .' (13:20, 21, NIV.)

Though the place was pure wilderness it continued to fascinate scholars because of its importance in Old Testament history and New Testament imagery. Major excavations began in 1899. The archaeologist Robert Koldeway received generous sponsorship from Imperial Germany. City walls, temples, palaces and houses were uncovered. Scores of baskets full of pottery and cartloads of stone carvings with cuneiform inscriptions were removed for study. Almost all dated from the period 626-539BC: *the reign of Nebuchadnezzar*. Accounts were discovered of Nebuchadnezzar's victorious campaigns against the Assyrians and Egyptians, *and of his annexation of Judah*. Babylonian inscriptions dovetailed with the biblical narrative.

From the discoveries in Babylon it has been possible to reconstruct the glory of this once massively beautiful city with its hanging gardens. Fascinating artefacts are to be found in the British

Museum and the State Museum in Berlin.

The Greek historian Herodotus says that the Babylonian king overlaid the walls of his great temple with gold, providing a great gold-plated bed and throne for his god. Two gold statues of Marduk were there, one sitting, one standing. Twenty tons of gold were used for the temple and its furniture. '*You are that head of gold*,' Daniel told Nebuchadnezzar when he expounded the image-vision (Daniel 2:38, NIV). Nebuchadnezzar would have latched on immediately. His was the *city* of gold.

A great processional way divided Babylon in half. Inscribed on paving stones and bricks was this legend: 'I am Nebuchadnezzar, King of Babylon, son of Nabopolassar, King of Babylon.' Nebuchadnezzar wanted present and posterity to know to whose glory that magnificent city was built. His claim was reflected in the pages of Scripture: ' "*Is not this the great Babylon I have built . . . , by my mighty power and for the glory of my majesty?*" ' (Daniel 4:30, NIV.)

His achievement was great; but in the perspective of history his boast rings hollow. Not only did his city remain a scene of desolation for thousands of years, but biblical critics laughed off Nebuchadnezzar and his grandson, Belshazzar, as figures of myth and folklore.

Until Koldeway's discoveries, that is, obliged them to be silent.

The long road to Nineveh

Claudius Rich had no difficulty in identifying Babylon. The ruined mound in Lower Mesopotamia was still called Tell Babil.

But what of Nineveh, capital of the mighty Assyrian Empire? Nineveh, whose might had to be brought down to make way for Babylon?

The site of Nineveh appeared to have been completely lost. In 1836 someone published Rich's records. He had, it appeared, explored a site near Mosul called Tell Nebi Yunus, The Mound of the Prophet Jonah. From Jonah's association with Nineveh, the pre-archaeologists leapt to the conclusion that the twin mounds of Tell Nebi Yunus and Kuyunjik, on the Tigris river opposite to modern Mosul, marked the site of the ancient Assyrian capital.

Paul Emile Botta, with financial backing from the French government, began excavations of a sort in 1842. But before cuneiform had been deciphered he was working in the dark, unable to assess the significance of his discoveries.

While Botta's army of diggers was at work, a man from the village of *Khorsabad*, who regularly passed their excavations, began to take an interest. If it was inscriptions and sculptures they were after, he told them, then they could do worse than visit *Khorsabad*. His home village was actually built on top of a mound (tell) and people were constantly coming across inscribed limestone slabs.

Botta sent a couple of his senior men to check out the suggestion. Within minutes of their arrival at *Khorsabad* they unearthed a number of large, beautifully carved slabs of stone. Within a month Botta had transferred his entire party to the new tell.

The work on *Khorsabad* began in 1843. Within two years Botta's discoveries were hogging the headlines. The vast palace of an Assyrian king was excavated. *Which* Assyrian king, they did not know, since they could not read the cuneiform inscriptions. But Botta was sure it was Nineveh. That is what he told the world. For a considerable period he was believed. What other city could yield such huge bas-reliefs – vast winged and human-headed lions and bulls, inscriptions galore, as well as *objects d'art* and weapons of war?

Only when Sir Henry Rawlinson had completely deciphered the Behistun inscription was it possible to say for sure that Botta was wrong.

But Botta had made huge collections of inscriptions. Rawlinson and his students were able to ascertain what Botta *had* found.

The city under *Khorsabad* and the palace it contained were soon identified. The palace had been that of Sargon II, Sennacherib's father. Sargon, Botta was told, was the conqueror of Samaria, capital of the Northern Kingdom of Israel. And he had left a detailed account of his conquest in cuneiform: 'I besieged and conquered Samaria and led away as booty 27,290 inhabitants of it.' What Sargon does *not* explain is that he was a general working under Shalmaneser V (see 2 Kings 18) at the time of the three campaigns against Samaria. Hence, in *his* annals, Shalmaneser claims to have conquered Samaria too!

The discovery of all this gave a black eye to those sceptical of Bible accuracy. Until these discoveries the names Sargon and Shalmaneser – like Nebuchadnezzar and Belshazzar – had not existed outside the Bible. 'Mythical characters', the sceptics had said. Botta might not have found Nineveh, but he 'found Sargon' and Sargon's palace, together with a detailed record of conquests which corroborated the biblical account. And soon he had 'found Shalmaneser' too!

From Botta's finds, Rawlinson drew the first reference to a king of Israel. Israel was referred to as 'the land of Omri'. Omri was the founder of a strong dynasty which included Ahab, and was the northern king responsible for moving the capital to Samaria.

Khorsabad was not built over Nineveh but over a veritable treasure-house of archaeological finds that have still to be exhausted. Sargon's palace with its gigantic winged bulls has now been completely excavated. On its walls are reliefs of battles and scenes of pomp and splendour, together with a comprehensive list of the kings of Assyria (indispensable to the archaeologist).

The search for Nineveh had proved fruitful in terms of biblical archaeology. But where *was* Nineveh?

Henry Layard had been pursuing yet another dead-end road to Nineveh. Instead he found *Nimrud*, a city built by Nimrod and known in Scripture as *Calah* (Genesis 10:11).

Again it was Rawlinson's 'decoding' of the cuneiform that disabused the hopeful explorer. Layard was compensated, to some extent, by the discovery among the debris of centuries of a giant monument which, in the face of the disapproval of the Turkish authorities, he shipped to the British Museum. Here it now resides in splendour: a great winged human-headed lion. Another pointer to the brilliance of the empire of which Nineveh was the capital.

That was only one exciting discovery at *Nimrud*.

Layard uncovered the Black Obelisk of Shalmaneser III (now in the British Museum). Carved into the hard black stone were five sections of reliefs and inscriptions. With Rawlinson's help, another reference to a Hebrew king was found: 'Jehu the son of Omri.' The adjacent relief depicted Jehu, among other subject kings, paying tribute to an Assyrian official.

As Layard's diggers worked on at *Nimrud*, the ruins of the palaces, large dwelling-houses and administrative buildings of a prosperous city were laid bare. Winged animals, distinctive of Assyrian sculpture, lined the walls. After Layard's time, monuments to the great Assyrian kings were discovered, together with a large number of carved ivory plaques. That ivory aroused much interest.

The biblical record refers to Ahab's palace '*inlaid with ivory*' (1 Kings 22:39, NIV). Archaeologists have made the assumption that the ivory found at the palace at *Nimrud* might well have been part of the loot brought from Samarian after its fall. During Dame Kathleen Kenyon's excavation of Samaria, in more recent times, ivory objects were found identical to those discovered years before at *Nimrud* in Iraq.

In 1989 *Nimrud* yielded more treasures, including a vast wealth of jewellery and the tomb of Yabahya, daughter of Sargon II.

But where was Nineveh? Why was it proving so elusive?

The decipherment of cuneiform script was what enabled scholars to plot the location of Nineveh. It lay opposite to present-day Mosul. Botta had made a false judgement in allowing himself to be lured away from the twin mounds of *Kuyunjik* and *Nebi Yujus* to the treasure-house at *Khorsabad*. Under the twin mounds were the old palaces and temples of Nineveh.

Under the mound of *Kuyunjik* the Library of Ashurbanipal was discovered. Literally tens of thousands of cuneiform documents, some historical, some literary, gave an insight into a rich and lavish civilisation.

At last Nineveh had been discovered. And what a discovery! In 1854, throughout the civilised world, newspapers carried the story that Rassam had found at Nineveh an ancient Babylonian legend of creation strongly reminiscent of the book of Genesis: The Gilgamesh Epic. Nineveh again hit the headlines in 1871 when George Smith, a journalist employed by the *Daily Telegraph*, discovered the Gilgamesh Flood Epic which also paralleled the flood story in Genesis.

On the tablets in the Library of Ashurbanipal, Nineveh, were found the names of a variety of Bible characters including Ahab, Hezekiah, Sennacherib, Sargon and many others.

Among the discoveries was a description of ancient Nineveh. It was described as a quadrangle, measuring a 150 x 90 stadia, with a total perimeter of 480 stadia, or about 60 miles. Hence it is still being excavated! Among the fortified walls discovered has been one of seven-and-a-half miles in length. Clearly Nineveh went far beyond the twin mounds of *Kuyunjik* and *Nebi Yunus*. Two gates have been excavated and partly restored. A royal palace has been excavated.

The biblical record indicates that, at the height of its power, Nineveh had a population of 120,000 (Jonah 4:11). Making a comparison between the area ancient Nineveh occupied with that covered by modern Mosul, which has a population of 100,000, we find that the biblical figures certainly appear realistic.

In 612BC Nineveh fell to the combined might of the Medes and the Babylonians. The fortifications were demolished and the palaces and temples were razed. The greater part of the population was slaughtered without mercy.

The total annihilation of Nineveh had been forecast in a Bible prophecy (Nahum 3:1-3, 5-7, 19).

Two hundred years after the fall of Nineveh, Greek historian and military leader Xenophon, with an army of 10,000, marched along the Tigris river after the Battle of Kunaxa. He caught sight of the landscape littered with heaps of ruins that had once been Nineveh. Xenophon asked the name of that great city of old. Those living near the site tendered their most humble apologies to the great general. The name of that city, they said, had been completely forgotten.

What happened to the Hittites?

Samaria was under siege from the Syrians. The hordes of Damascus had the capital of the Northern Kingdom at their mercy. Massive carnage was expected.

Then, overnight, a rumour spread through the Syrian camp. The King of Israel, it was said, had made an alliance with the King of the Hittites. That caused such terror among the Syrian army that they fled and the siege came to an unaccountable end (2 Kings 7).

This is just one of the Old Testament references to a powerful people called the Hittites. From the Old Testament context it is clear that the Hittites represented one of the super powers over a period of many centuries. It is equally clear that individual Hittite families were permitted to live at peace in the Israelite kingdoms and that Hittite commanders held positions of honour close to Israelite kings.

In the eighteenth and nineteenth centuries the Hittites were a source of considerable embarrassment to both Christian and Jewish scholars. Despite the high profile of Hittites in the Old Testament, there was no reference to such a people anywhere else. On no subject did the scholars intent on discrediting the biblical record render themselves more insufferable. 'The Hittites? Who were the Hittites? There were no such people as the Hittites! The Hittites were never mentioned by classical historians. Therefore, there *were* no Hittites. The Bible had to be untrue. Just another example of a fabled people produced by a fecund imagination.'

Once again the dogmatic critics were to end up with egg on

their faces. So much egg, in fact, that if such bold assertions had been made in any other academic discipline than biblical criticism – and then been so conclusively confounded – there would have had to be many resignations from important positions in the universities and in the churches. However, there is no record that any such resignations occurred when, to quote English scholar A. H. Sayce, 'All of a sudden we were digging up Hittites all over the place!'

In fact the rediscovery of the Hittites began in 1876. At first it was largely the work of Sayce. *En route* between his houseboat on the Nile and Oxford University where, each spring, Sayce gave a series of lectures, he passed through the Near East. At Hama and Aleppo in Syria he found picture-writing on stone blocks reused in medieval buildings. Passing on through Turkey he found the same kind of writing carved on rocks. In 1876 he made a positive connection between these writings, the Hittites of the Old Testament, and the *Kheta* named in Egyptian texts.

The *Kheta* were one of the 'great powers' of the history inscribed in ancient Egyptian stone. It had been a source of puzzlement for archaeologists for many years to know who the *Kheta* were. One *Kheta* king, for example, had made a treaty with Pharaoh Rameses II.

It was clear from the account of that treaty that the pharaoh and the king had made the treaty as equals. Where could a nation be found as powerful as that of the Egyptians at the height of their supremacy?

From 1876 the scholarly world had the answer to that question. An answer that had its origins, at first, in those strange hieroglyphic inscriptions in Syria and Turkey.

A. H. Sayce and W. Wright successfully dated the Hittite inscriptions to the centuries between 1600 and 700BC. However, not until 1947, as a result of the work of Bossert, was hieroglyphic Hittite fully understood. Bossert found bilingual inscriptions – and suddenly the history of the Hittites was available to be read.

Long before 1947, however, it was realised that the Hittites were, in fact, a major power. Between 1906 and 1912 the Hittite capital *Hattushash* – now called Boghazkoy – was excavated by

Hugo Winckler. The site was one hundred miles due east of Ankara, Turkey. Much of the Hittite city was above ground and, for years, the locals had been selling clay tablets as souvenirs to foreign visitors.

In the course of his excavations Winckler was fortunate enough to stumble upon the archives of the Hittite royal family. The tablets were written in cuneiform Hittite, a script used by the Hittites in addition to their hieroglyphic system of writing. Because of its similarity to Babylonian cuneiform, Hittite cuneiform was deciphered as early as 1915 by Czech scholar Hrozny. Ten thousand tablets containing cuneiform Hittite were found in the royal archives at *Hattushash*. Fascinating for those already aware of the treaty with Ramases II was the discovery of the Hittite copy of the same treaty!

From the tablets of the royal archives emerged a chronology of Middle Eastern history, and the role played by the Hittites in it, during the period 1400-1200BC. In addition there was a complete record of the Hittite kings during that period. It was clear that the Hittites were a civilised people and that their scribes were capable of writing in seven different languages (variants of cuneiform).

The excavation of the Hittite capital *Hattushash* was completed during the 1950s. It was a city of 300 acres. It was a well-constructed city of stone and brick, with more or less impregnable defences. On its east side was a high rock which had served as a fortified citadel. Within the city area five temples were uncovered. In the royal archives details had already been deciphered of the worship ritual of the Hittites, much being made in learned journals of their elaborate and lengthy religious services.

These details of a heathen system of worship, in themselves, were of considerable interest. The critics had previously claimed that the Hebrew laws of Exodus, Leviticus, Numbers and Deuteronomy were too 'advanced' (complicated) to be dated in Moses' time. The *Hattushash* Tablets, together with tablets excavated in other Hittite cities, revealed a heathen system of worship equally as complex as that of Israel under Moses.

The symbol of the Hittites was the lion. Great lions stood on either side of the gateway to *Hattushash*.

Hittite cities and satellite states in northern Syria came to light. These were the cities with which Solomon had traded (1 Kings 10:29). Among them were *Zenjirli* and *Carchemish*.

It has been ascertained that the rise of the Hittites to major power status began in 1750BC and that, although they continued to have significant and cultural influence beyond that date, the sun had effectively set on the Hittite empire by about 1200BC.

The *Encyclopaedia Britannica* devoted only eight lines to the Hittites in the 1860 edition. The 1947 edition of the same encyclopaedia was obliged to devote over ten full pages of two columns each to an article dealing with Hittite history, culture, and religion.

Evidently the Hittites were not one of the Bible's 'historical mistakes'.

Creation and the Flood

The discovery at Nineveh of the Gilgamesh Epics turned the attention of Bible scholars to the early chapters of Genesis. The Creation Epic (discovered in 1854) and the Flood Epic (discovered in 1871) closely paralleled the Bible accounts.

There was a conscious search for other cuneiform accounts of the Creation and the Flood. In 1915 the oldest of all the Creation epics was found. The six-column *stele*, known as the Sumerian Epic, was dated to around 2350BC. It mirrored the Genesis account of Creation to a surprising degree.

Babylonian accounts of the Deluge were discovered. They even contained the names of kings and dynasties which reigned *before* the Flood.

Ur of the Chaldees

Sir Leonard Woolley's excavation of Ur of the Chaldees provided remarkable insights. That city, near the Gulf, was the one left behind by Abraham and his family.

Those biblical critics who had not relegated Abraham to the land of legend had him down as an illiterate sheikh, who had deserted a primitive settlement to chase superstitions through the desert.

As Woolley's findings were released during the 1920s, quite a large battalion of 'higher critics' were having to find something else to talk about.

What Woolley dug up was a populous city with large buildings — *so* large they presupposed the use of some strong means of leverage like a crane — which had served as a political and cultural centre 4,000 and more years previously.

Ur had the most impressive *ziggurat* or temple tower of the Mesopotamian region. Even after four millennia in ruins it measured seventy feet high. It was constructed with well-baked bricks. Almost every brick had an inscription. From those inscriptions Woolley's team read the history of the whole region.

The name Abraham was identified on contract tablets dating from around 2000BC. Among the witnesses to such contracts appear names like Jacob, Terah, Sarah, Milcah and Laban.

The city contained other temples.

There was an impressive residential quarter. Typically the houses were two storey, with a street door and a rear door leading to a central patio enclosed by kitchens, store rooms and capacious living rooms. Ur had been served by an efficient underground sanitation system (which puts to shame the sanitation arrangements in most towns of present-day Iraq).

Several schools were excavated. Cuneiform tablets were found in them. From these tablets it was clear that the wealthier classes in Ur — and, because of the size of his flocks and herds, Abraham must have been included among them — had a sophisticated grasp of maths, trigonometry, astronomy and geography.

The date of the Exodus

How we interpret the archaeological finds in Egypt very much depends on whether we date the Exodus in the fifteenth century or the thirteenth century BC.

As has been indicated in our dating of the Pentateuch (chapter 2), we believe the fifteenth century date to be accurate. The reasons are both biblical and archaeological.

1 Kings 6:1 is a vital reference point for biblical chronology: '*In the four hundred and eightieth year after the Israelites had come out of Egypt, in the fourth year of Solomon's reign over Israel, in the month of Ziv, the second month, he began to build the temple of the Lord.*' (NIV.) That Solomon began to build his temple

in the year 967BC is not disputed. Hence the date of the Exodus must have been around 1450BC. The Pharaoh of the Oppression is taken as Thutmoses III. The Pharaoh of the Exodus is taken as Amenhotep II (1450-1425BC). The period of the wilderness wanderings is taken to be *circa* 1450-*circa* 1410BC. And the period thereafter as the years of Joshua's conquest of Canaan.

Among the difficulties of the thirteenth century Exodus under Pharaoh Ramses II is that it places Joshua two centuries before Moses! And distorts the biblical narrative in all kinds of ways. The 1450BC date for the Exodus harmonises with God's prophecy to Abraham that the Israelites would serve for 400 years until his plan was ripe for them to occupy Canaan (Genesis 15:13-16). If the period is understood to extend from Abraham, it also harmonises with the 430 years mentioned in Exodus 12:40 (see footnote in NIV).

The 'late date' view was widely held in the mid-nineteenth century. By the 1890s the 'early date' was gaining support. Authorities including Max Muller (1897), James Breasted (1897), H. R. R. Hall and A. H. Gardiner (1913), E. Peet (1922), C. A. F. Knight (1922), J. W. Jack (1925), J. Garstang (1931), T. H. Robinson (1932), A. S. Yahuda (1933), W. J. Phythian-Adams (1934), E. O. James (1935), W. A. F. Blunt (1936), A. Bradford (1936), S. L. Craiger (1936), and Siegfried Horn (1953 and 1978), among others, believed that biblical data taken together with the discovery of the Israel *stele* and the evidence of the Tell el Amarna tablets make the 'late date' view untenable.

However, certain modern Egyptologists who take the *late date* view assert, on the basis of it, that there is no archaeological evidence for the Exodus from Egypt. Hence it has become fashionable to doubt whether the Exodus ever actually occurred. Is there archaeological evidence for the Exodus if one accepts the *early date* view?

There is, we believe, archaeological evidence not only for the *early date* Exodus, but for Joseph's contribution to Egyptian history.

Joseph was sold into Egypt about 1847BC. The transaction occurred at Dothan where Joseph was thrown into a pit or cistern; a tell identified as Dothan has been excavated with a deep cistern at the foot of the gradient.

The sale of Joseph by the Midianite traders to Potiphar is paralleled by many records of *Kan'amu* (Canaanite) slaves. Names like Potiphar are of genuine Egyptian origin. Ankle-length examples of the *'coat of many colours'* are found in pictures of semitic visitors to Egypt. The *'signet ring'*, the *'vesture of fine linen'*, and the *'gold chain about Joseph's neck'* to which the Bible refers all accord with Egyptian custom.

The biblical record indicates that Joseph predicted to Pharaoh that there would be *'seven years of plenty'* and *'seven years of famine'*, and asserts that he was appointed to the office of *merper* or *vizier* to make appropriate preparations. That incident is likely to have taken place towards the beginning of the Twelfth Dynasty, perhaps under Pharaoh Sesostris I. Sesostris was the pharaoh who built the first large obelisk called the Pillar of On. The Bible indicates that Joseph married the daughter of the priest of On.

The important office to which Sesostris appointed Joseph and the accoutrements of that office, are often mentioned in inscriptions. Doubt was once cast on the possibility of a mere Canaanite slave's promotion to high honours in Egypt. But archaeology has discovered many striking parallels. Neri-Ra, a Canaanite, became armour-bearer to Pharaoh. Ben-Mat-Ana, also a Canaanite, was raised to the important office of interpreter. Yankhamu, a semite, actually became deputy to Pharaoh Amenhotep III with a charge over the granaries of the Delta.

The Bible indicates that Sesostris gave the order that everyone should 'bow the knee' to Joseph. That detail puzzled the experts for some time. Normally the people would not bow to a *vizier*. But archaeology has turned up evidence of such a *vizier* under Sesostris I. The vizier's name, according to the inscription, was Min-tu-ho-tip. In the early Twelfth Dynasty a canal, still known as *Bahr Yusuf* (Joseph's Canal), was dug, possibly as part of his preparation for the famine years.

The Tomb of Amani dates from the reign of Sesostris I. On the wall of this tomb is a record in hieroglyphs of how Amani helped prepare for a coming famine, and how, through good management, Egypt survived the famine well.

An early Eighteenth Dynasty pharaoh, perhaps Thutmoses I, was the 'new king over Egypt, which knew not Joseph' (Exodus 1:8). A spirit of ethnic consciousness would appear to have been fostered. That was not the first time that there had been such an upsurge, and that foreigners had borne the brunt of the quasi-nationalistic spirit. A century earlier – in 1567BC – the Asiatic *Hyksos* had been expelled from Egypt.

The suspicion and hatred against the semitic Israelites which had begun under Thutmoses I was continued during the short reign of his successor, Thutmoses II, the fourth ruler of the Eighteenth Dynasty.

The untimely death of Thutmoses II left his widow Hatshepsut as *de facto* ruler. From 1504 to 1482BC she ruled with a strong but steady hand. She built a grandiose mortuary-temple at Deir el-Bahri in western Thebes, still considered by many to be the most beautiful of the Egyptian temples.

The character of Hatshepsut gained from the Bible is not unlike that of the historical Hatshepsut. Both chronology and historical circumstances point to her as the foster mother of Moses. Records indicate that she hated Thutmoses III, her nephew, who had been foisted on her as a co-ruler (but whom she successfully kept in the background for many years). She might well have intended Moses as her successor. Josephus Flavius connects this princess of the House of Thutmoses with the 'princess' who found Moses 'in the bulrushes' (Exodus 2:5 et seq).

In naming the baby as she did, she conferred upon him a name common in her family. Since she had found him in the river it might have been in her mind to name him after the river god, Hapi. It is probable that she called him Hapi-moses, 'Born of the God Hapi'. Later Moses would reject the name of the Egyptian god. Hence his name simply meant 'Born of'.

From the beginning of her reign Hatshepsut announced her intention of reigning as a man. That may be the reason why many representations have her in male attire. In addition to the many temples and obelisks which survive to this day, she erected the Giant Obelisk (100 feet) at Karnak.

Whatever Hatshepsut's plans had been for Moses, he mysteriously disappeared from the scene. It is likely that by that time Hatshepsut's strong-minded ways had excited the jealousy of her overshadowed co-ruler, Thutmoses III. At all events, as soon as she was dead he began a policy of defacing the monuments she had erected.

The death of Hatshepsut inaugurated the last and worst phase of the oppression of the Israelites. Thutmoses III reigned as sole ruler for thirty-three years (1482-1450BC). He had the reputation of a merciless tyrant and conducted successful military campaigns in Palestine and Syria. The most important historical monument to Thutmoses III is his famous inscription on a pylon of the Temple at Karnak. Here we find the earliest references to Canaan in the Egyptian royal inscriptions. It describes the conquests of Thutmoses III, and names, familiar from the Bible story, recur, including Kadesh, Megiddo, Dothan, Damascus, Hazor, Carmel, Joppa, Gath and Bethel. Among the place-names recorded on that monument are two which have special interest for us: Joseph-El and Jacob-Er. Scholars are uneasy about suggesting that those names have anything to do with the biblical Joseph or Jacob. Nevertheless their occurrence at that point in time is interesting.

The successor of Thutmoses III, Amenhotep II (1450-1425BC), was probably the pharaoh of the Exodus. His reputation for cruelty equalled that of his predecessor.

Near the pyramid of Sesostris II, a city was excavated by Sir Flinders Petrie in 1891. Rosalie David published a book in 1986 highlighting some of Petrie's discoveries; *among them, that the entire city was occupied by semitic slaves.* Following the 'late date' Exodus theory, Rosalie David does not make the connection between that excavation and the Israelites of the Bible. She does, however, recount one of Petrie's discoveries germane to the biblical record; underneath the floors of many houses were boxes containing the skeletons of babies a few months old at death. That may or may not be connected with the policy pursued by Pharaoh and described in Exodus 1:11-22. Even more interesting was Rosalie David's assertion that the departure of the semitic slaves was 'sudden and unpremeditated'. That slaves could simply pack up and leave is puzzling, unless you accept the biblical account.

The conquest of Canaan

At the time of the Exodus the centre of the Egyptian Empire seemed as firm as ever. Its circumference, however, began to show signs of breaking up as Pharaoh Amenhotep the Magnificent's luxury-sodden reign progressed. A letter to Burna-Buriash, King of Babylon, *circa* 1380BC, speaks of disaffection among the vassal kings of Canaan in the reign of his father (which included the years 1410-1400BC). The Tell el Amarna Tablets describe a tumultuous situation in the 1400 period.

Tel el Amarna is situated on the Upper Nile. In 1887 someone living there began poking about in a rubbish heap. There he uncovered a collection of inscribed clay tablets. In the months that came after, hundreds of these tablets were destroyed by ignorant, over-eager 'excavators'.

The scholars arrived in time to rescue 300 of them.

After considerable study these tablets turned out to be the buried records of the once-royal capital of *Akhnaton*. The tablets were, in effect, letters and despatches sent out during the years 1380-1360BC to the Egyptian court.

Most of the tablets had been written by kings of Canaanite cities named in the Bible – including the King of Jerusalem – and written *to* the pharaohs.

All the letters were written in Babylonian cuneiform. Since both the Canaanites and the Egyptians had a well-developed language and alphabet of their own, it would appear that they were using this form of cuneiform as the language of diplomacy.

The letters reveal that Canaan, a province of the Egyptian Empire, was in a state of extreme turmoil.

The vassal kings were sending frenzied appeals to the pharaohs. They needed help! Formidable invaders were coming from both the north and the east.

The invaders from the north were the restless Hittites. However, the Tell el Amarna Tablets make clear that the dreaded Hittite invasion of the heart of Canaan never materialised. Happenings elsewhere in their northern empire diverted Hittite attention, and their forces withdrew — leaving Canaan wide open to the Israelite forces attacking from the east.

Among the Tell el Amarna Tablets are the letters of Arad-Hiba, King of Jerusalem, complaining to Pharaoh of the depredations of a people called the *Habiru*. Elsewhere in the *Tell el Amarna* record we read: 'The Habiru are now capturing the fortresses of the Pharaoh. Not a single governor remains among them to my lord the King: all have perished. . . . The land of the King is lost to the Habirus. . . .'

The identification of the *Habiru* as the Hebrews is, perhaps, an obvious one. More especially since the circumstances of the *Habiru* invasion from the east are precisely those of the Hebrew invasion, as regards date, location, results and the actual place names concerned.

The Tell el Amarna Tablets are painting from the Canaanite side the same picture which the historian of the biblical books of Joshua and Judges paints from the Hebrew side.

The Tel el Amarna Tablets present one difficulty, however. It is next to impossible to identify cuneiform names from their context. Hence it is disappointing, at first sight, that no biblical personal names are identified with certainty. It is also beyond question that the tablets date from the period immediately *after* Joshua's initial incursion into Canaan. Hence they are largely concerned with the battles fought and won by his successors.

The fall of Jericho

The first Canaanite city to fall to Joshua's armies was Jericho. The Bible account describes how Jericho's walls fell and how, thereafter, the city was gutted by fire.

Jericho represents one of the most impressive tells in Palestine. Archaeologists have discovered from it that Jericho's greatest days were over long before the Israelite armies surrounded it.

During the age of scientific archaeology the tell Jericho has been subjected to two intensive excavations.

The first of these was undertaken by Professor John Garstang and his team between 1930 and 1936. Garstang grabbed the headlines and shook the critics when he published his finds. In many parts of the tell he found the stumps of walls, clear evidence that the major part of the walls had 'fallen down'. While the critics sniggered, Garstang and his team persisted. There were two walls, parallel, with a space of fifteen feet between them. Buildings had rested across the tops of those walls. A violent conflagration had overtaken the city, completely destroying it. Garstang dated that conflagration to 1400BC, a date he reached on the evidence of Egyptian scarabs from tombs he opened around Jericho. This accorded with the 'early date' for the Exodus and the Conquest.

The second excavation of Jericho was headed by Dr Kathleen Kenyon and took place between 1952 and 1958. With others she had believed that there was something 'too good to be true' about Garstang's findings. She applied her trench system to Jericho and, after some years of research, began to publish her findings.[1]

Immediately those in the popular press who scented a 'good story' polarised the findings of Garstang and the findings of Kenyon. Kenyon, it was reported, dated the truncated walls to a period before the Israelite conquest and asserted that erosion by the elements made it impossible to find any traces of Joshua's Jericho.

Certainly Dame Kathleen was more sceptical about the evidence than Garstang had been. Nevertheless, in her book *Archaeology in the Holy Land*,[2] she conceded that Jericho had been destroyed by fire, that there was widespread evidence of the fire-scorched stumps of walls to which Garstang had referred, and that the destruction had covered an area about 56 feet by

24 feet. In addition she found evidence of a partial rebuilding programme in Jericho, undertaken in the historical period which – if we accept the 'early date' Conquest – would have followed Joshua's destruction. Despite that, in the most recent revision of her book *The Bible and Recent Archaeology*,[3] it is made crystal clear that Dr Kenyon did not associate what she found with the biblical narrative.

Dame Kathleen found evidence of widespread destruction in different parts of Palestine dating from the same period. That destruction affected cities as far apart as the metropolis of Hazor, north of Galilee; and Lachish, south of Jerusalem. Kenyon attributed that destruction to the Asiatic *Hyksos* and two Egyptian attempts to reassert control in Canaan. According to the biblical narrative the cities, including Hazor and Lachish, at that time blackened by destruction, were taken by Joshua's forces. It is, therefore, possible that the damage she attributes to the *Hyksos* and the Egyptians was in fact inflicted by the Israelites.

In 1990 American archaeologist Professor Bryant Wood reported new and important information about the destruction of Jericho. He had been studying the excavation reports of Kenyon that were published after her death. He found that she had misdated pottery from the last major city of Jericho. She had dated it 1550BC, having looked for foreign, painted pottery and found it to be absent. She had failed to recognise the now better-known local pottery which existed in profusion in the final destruction level of the tell. In addition Professor Wood actually found some of the very painted pottery in Garstang's pottery bags in the Louvre that Kenyon had missed. Wood's findings were published in the *Biblical Archaeology Reviews* for 1990. Hence the findings at Jericho fit the biblical account even better than anyone previously recognised. Everything points to 1400BC as the date of Jericho's destruction.

Professor Garstang believed that down to 1360BC there was considerable archaeological evidence to corroborate the settlement of Canaan by the Israelites. But from that date until the coming of the Philistines, 200 years later, we are left very much in the dark. The Bible itself provides very little detail.

Tablets discovered at Beth-shan in 1923 provide evidence of a Hittite attack on Hazor – a city which Joshua had acknowledged as the strategic key to the control of the northlands – *and* contain the first Egyptian attempts to reproduce the name *Habiru* or Hebrew.

The Israel Stele

The Israel *Stele* was discovered by Sir Flinders Petrie in 1896. Conveniently it is self-dated in 'the third year of Merenptah' [1223BC].

The Israel *Stele* contains a great deal of valuable information which corroborates the biblical narrative. In addition it is the first 'document' outside the Bible on which the actual name *Israel* appears.

The obvious conclusion from that is that by the thirteenth century the Israelites were well settled in Canaan and were known by foreign powers to be its rulers.

The Philistines

Kenyon wrote, 'About the year 1200BC there was a catastrophic interruption in the civilisation of the whole of the eastern Mediterranean, producing a Dark Age very like that following the Roman Empire in Europe 1,600 years later, and brought about by similar events, the incursions of barbarian groups.'[4]

The barbarians came from the sea and very nearly wrested the promised land from the Israelites. The Philistines are believed to have come from the Aegean Islands by way of Crete. They attacked Egypt, Palestine, and the Hittite country. Though they failed to force their way into Egypt, they successfully settled on the maritime plain of Palestine.

Evidence of Philistine destruction has been excavated at Askelon, Ashdod and Ekron.

Old Jerusalem

Excavation of Old Jerusalem commenced under the Palestine Exploration Fund in 1865. The original city of Jerusalem was on the Hill Ophel, a spur running south of Temple Mount. Dr Kenyon asserted, however, that part of Israelite Jerusalem was under the present-day Old City. She predicted that as people excavated beneath their homes they would dig up the ancient past. That has proved to be the case.

But most concerted excavation has centred on the Hill Ophel, flanked by steep slopes with the Kidron Valley to the east and the Tyropoeon Valley to the west. These steep valleys, together with the proximity of a water source, the Gihon Spring, account for the original settlement.

The Palestine Exploration Fund excavators found traces of an original occupation dating back as far as 3000BC. As a walled city Ophel seems to have been fortified just prior to 2000BC.

Between 1923 and 1925 a portion of wall on the eastern crest of Ophel was excavated. Prior to David's conquest the name of the city had been *Jebus*. The Jebusite walls, and signs of the breach made by David's well-known assault upon the place, can still be seen. More interesting still, a combination of tunnels, including a vertical shaft, was discovered. That had given the Jebusites their access to water. The vertical shaft had been that up which Joab and his men had crawled to take the defenders in the rear, and for David to take a town the Jebusites had believed impregnable (1 Chronicles 11:5, 6). The shaft has usually been known by the name of its discoverer, Warren's Shaft.

During the 1960s further excavations were launched by the British School of Archaeology. More walls were discovered, some dating from the Jebusite period, others from the davidic period. Some made a distinction between the rough and hasty masonry associated with David, and the more carefully dressed stones of Solomon's period.

It was on Temple Mount – the Mount Moriah of earlier biblical history – that Solomon built his palace and his vast temple. The fact that, in a later age, Herod the Great covered the whole area with a vast platform, and that that platform is now occupied by Muslim shrines has prevented meaningful excavation, though a few rooms, stables and cisterns have been discovered beneath the present-day paved area. Of the palace and the temple there are no certain traces.

The divided kingdoms

With the death of Solomon – *circa* 970BC – came the division of the kingdoms. The northern tribes rebelled against the luxuries and excesses of Solomon's Jerusalem and then, ironically, patterned their Northern Kingdom of Israel on Solomon's reign. In the Southern Kingdom of Judah, including Jerusalem, where the luxurious excesses had taken place, there was a reaction. The Southern Kingdom of Judah went back to the simplicity of an earlier period.

Solomon had fortified the northern city of Megiddo (1 Kings 9:15). There shades of his magnificence can be seen in the Tell Megiddo. To uncover signs of magnificence in the period after Solomon's death we must look exclusively north of the frontier between Judah and Israel.

The earlier kings of the north had no fixed abode. Their first base was *Shechem* (Nablus). Then their capital was transferred to *Tirzah* (at the time of Baasha, the third king). About 885BC Omri laid siege to Tirzah, captured it and the usurper Zimri, and made plans to build a new capital elsewhere. Excavations by the *Ecole Biblique* have identified the *Tell el Far'ah* as Tirzah. The evidence of Omri's violent destruction is there in abundance; the contents of the houses are buried in the debris of their superstructures.

From this period on, the important archaeological evidence changes. At long last we find contemporary inscriptions which deal explicitly with Hebrew history. We recognise familiar Bible names and situations in independent records written by men who were actually contemporaries of Elijah, Amos and Isaiah. The inscriptions, however, whether on stone or clay, were prepared by potentates with one eye on posterity and the other on immediate self-glorification. But, for all that, they are most illuminating.

Omri, King of Israel, 886-874BC, is the first Hebrew king whose name appears in the monuments of antiquity. His name was chiselled on the Stone of Mesha and upon the cuneiform records of Assyria. That is an indication that the world was waking up to the importance of the Hebrews. Omri's reign is very lightly passed over in the Bible (1 Kings 16:23-28), but the independent records provide ample evidence that the impression that he made on his contemporaries was by no means small.

King Omri transferred the capital of Israel from *Tirzah* to Samaria (1 Kings 16:24). Kathleen Kenyon says that on the evidence of pottery, 'where Tell el Far'ah stops, Samaria begins'. She found evidence that Omri moved not only his court but, in all probability, all of the inhabitants, complete with all of their property.

The credit for the excavation of Samaria belongs to a Harvard expedition under Reisner in 1909, and, secondly, to a British expedition under Crofoot in the 1930s. Omri had grand ideas for Samaria. The excavated buildings and layout of the capital demonstrate that eloquently. The city had a good strategic situation, lying athwart the main north-south route, hence in easy contact with Phoenicia and in a position to spot and prevent any aggressive advances from Judah. It was to facilitate trade that Omri married his son Ahab to Jezebel of Tyre.

'Excavation confirms the biblical account that Omri founded his town on a virgin site,' writes Kenyon, who worked as an assistant to Crofoot. Samaria was laid out as a new city dominated by a royal quarter. In that it resembled Solomon's Jerusalem. The royal quarter was built on a 'summit plateau' above the level of the remainder of the city. The building of the city was extended and completed by Ahab who succeeded his father within six years of the move to the new capital.

The Assyrian menace loomed large during the reigns of both Omri and Ahab. The cuneiform record describing the Assyrian victory at the Battle of Karkar on the Shalmanezer's Monolith Inscription includes an important reference to Ahab, King of Israel, son of Omri. 1 Kings 22:39 refers to '*the ivory house*' built by Ahab. Excavations indicate that Ahab enlarged the palace built by his father and added a tremendously heavy double wall, completely encircling it, plus a massive royal treasury with an elaborate system of store chambers. Ivory wall plaques were excavated in Ahab's palace at Samaria in 1933. The same ivory had already been discovered in Sargon's palace in Nimrud, taken there after the fall of Samaria at the hands of the Assyrians.

The Omri-Ahab palace was Phoenician in style. Along with Jezebel, Ahab might also have imported Phoenician craftsmen.

The Moabite Stone, discovered in 1868, contains a royal inscription written in Hebrew. About three-and-a-half feet in height, two feet wide and two feet thick, the Moabite Stone with its inscription is of immense importance. It describes the historical situation: Omri had triumphed over Moab for '*many days*' before his death, and Ahab had inherited the tribute payable by Moab (2 Kings 3:4).

Cut off from worship at the temple in Jerusalem, the northern kings set up religious centres at the northern and southern extremities of their kingdom: Dan and Bethel. Excavations at the Tell Dan have shown that the same style of architecture was used as at Samaria. A rectangular summit (or high place) has been excavated, approached by a flight of steps. Many of the large public buildings at Megiddo belong to Ahab's reign. Among them was a southern palace. To Ahab's reign also belongs the huge water shaft at Megiddo, a major undertaking, providing direct access to the spring from the interior of the town. It consists of a vertical shaft 35 metres deep, plus a horizontal tunnel 63 metres long. The even more impressive water system at Hazor also belongs to Ahab's reign. In Hazor, as in Megiddo and Samaria, a royal-administrative quarter was built during Ahab's reign, separate from the residential quarters.

With Ahab employed in ambitious building projects, the Assyrian advance continued inexorably into the Northern Kingdom. After the accession of Tiglath-Pileser III in Nineveh the advance of Assyria was unstoppable. Any number of inscriptions bear out the record of the biblical books of Kings and Chronicles, as do the archaeological excavations of Dame Kathleen Kenyon. The end of Stratum IV at Megiddo represents the destruction brought about by the Assyrian attack *circa* 734BC. The violent destruction of Stratum V at Hazor is to be ascribed to the same cause. Dame Kathleen: 'On most sites there is, in fact, evidence of violent events during this period.'

The fall of the Southern Kingdom

The fall of the Northern Kingdom made a deep impression in Jerusalem. That is indicated by the reforms of Hezekiah and the increased influence of the prophetic schools in diplomatic affairs. For a time Isaiah completely controlled the policy of his king. He saw clearly that the real issue was between Assyria and Egypt, and that Judah's only hope of avoiding destruction lay in neutrality. The description of Isaiah (20:1) of Sargon's expedition against Ashdod is borne out and amplified in the Khorsabad Inscription and also in the Cylinder of Sargon discovered in Ashurbanipal's library at Nineveh.

In 705BC Sennacherib began to ravage Judah. Lachish was captured and sacked; the Bible describes it; archaeology authenticates it. Jerusalem was besieged but held out. Hezekiah bought off the Assyrians by paying tribute. Judah had bought time for another century but was, in effect, a semi-independent vassal. Dr Kenyon writes: 'On a number of sites archaeological evidence has been found of these events, for their effect was so cataclysmic that there is seldom much doubt in the correlation of the archaeological and historical (biblical) evidence.'[5]

Though Jerusalem did not fall to the Assyrians it was placed in desperate straits. Hezekiah and his masons became active. The town walls were repaired. Most importantly, Hezekiah and his engineers carried out a massive work of civil engineering. Hitherto the city had been dependent upon the Gihon Spring outside the walls and upon the rock-cisterns for rain-water. But then Hezekiah *'made a pool, and a conduit, and brought water into the city'* (2 Kings 20:20). Hezekiah's engineers built a tunnel through 1,800 feet of living rock from the Gihon Spring (outside the city wall) to the Pool of Siloam (well inside the city). That was of vital importance in withstanding a siege, more especially since Warren's Shaft had long been filled with rubble, forgotten and abandoned. The achievement was referred to several times in 2 Kings and 2 Chronicles.

Hezekiah's Tunnel has been known for a long period, but, in1880, Dr Conrad Schick discovered the Siloam Inscription when wading through the conduit under the walls of Old Jerusalem. The tunnel had been built by two separate groups of workmen chiselling from either end. The inscription records the excitement of the two parties of workmen as they met under the heart of the Hill Ophel. In the excavations of 1909-1911 the whole tunnel was cleared out.

In 621BC the Assyrian Empire gave way to the Babylonian Empire. Babylon conquered Assyrian territories. In campaigns in 598 and 589-587 Nebuchadnezzar finally annexed Judah. 'Archaeology fully supports the biblical evidence of the disastrous effect of the Babylonian campaign which brought this period to a close. Large numbers of towns were destroyed and never occupied again. Of these, Tell Beit Mirsim and Beth-Shemesh are typical examples.' Beersheba is another. The precise dating of the fall of these cities to the Babylonian armies can be pinpointed by pottery.[6]

Zedekiah's revolt against Nebuchadnezzar led to the final destruction of Jerusalem in 586BC (2 Kings 24:17-25). Nebuchadnezzar had inscriptions chiselled which are still extant and bear out the biblical records. The Jerusalem excavations undertaken between 1961 and 1967 uncovered evidence among the collapsed terraces, retaining walls and houses of the violence of the destruction.

Return from exile

In 540BC the Babylonian Empire was annexed by the Persians under Cyrus. The Persian Empire pursued a policy of toleration towards national cultures and religions. Evidence for this policy has been found in the Cylinder of Cyrus dating from 536BC.

Successive leaders led parties back to Jerusalem. In 520BC Zerubbabel rebuilt the temple, way down-market of the grand edifice of Solomon.

In 444BC Nehemiah and his masons restored the walls of the city. No new kingdom could grow up around the partially rebuilt Jerusalem. Many Jews, in fact, remained behind in Babylonia and Persia.

Those who returned were continually at loggerheads with

what Nehemiah calls *'the peoples of the land'*. The returned exiles despised these people as being of mixed blood. That was the beginning of the Samaritan schism. The occasion of that was when Manasseh, grandson of High Priest Eliashib, was driven out by Nehemiah on the grounds of intermarriage. Sanballat, governor of Samaria, built a temple on Mount Gerazim, a rival to the temple at Jerusalem.

Despite painstaking excavation between 1961 and 1967, little remains of Zerubbabel's second temple, except for the south-east corner of the temple platform. Nehemiah's walls, however, have proved more durable. A wall on the crest of Ophel, previously ascribed to an earlier period, was found to date from the period of Nehemiah's rebuilding.

The chief reason why so little of Zerubbabel's temple has survived: Herod the Great extended its area into a large platform and built a far grander edifice over it.

References:
[1] Kathleen Kenyon, *Archaeology in the Holy Land*, fourth edition, pages vii-ix, 5, 14, 328, 331-332.
[2] Ibid, pages 181 et seq.
[3] Kathleen Kenyon, *The Bible and Recent Archaeology*
(revised and partially rewritten by P.R.S. Moody in 1987), page 73.
[4] Kathleen Kenyon, *Archaeology in the Holy Land*, fourth edition, page 212.
[5] Ibid, page 288.
[6] Ibid, pages 296, 299.

Digging up the New Testament

Herod: the great builder

'Jesus was born in Bethlehem of Judaea in the days of King Herod.' (Matthew 2:1.) And this 'King Herod' – whose paranoid dynasty, from their cameo parts, provides a chill menace to the Gospel story – earned the epithet 'great' by his building enterprises.

'Herod was one of the most passionate builders of antiquity.'[1]

The hallmark of Herodian masonry: huge, oblong blocks of stone with smooth margins cut around a central, raised boss.

The elder Pliny wrote that Herod made Jerusalem 'the most famous of the great cities of the East'.

In 19BC Herod decided on the gargantuan task of rebuilding the Jerusalem temple. Acutely conscious that he was not a Jew, he needed to legitimise his reign in the eyes of Jewish leaders. He set out to ensure that *his* temple outshone Solomon's.

Herod's ten thousand workmen were instructed not to touch the old building. The temple services could not be interrupted while the structure of his imagination was erected. As much as possible of the most sacred part of the temple was prepared off the site before the one thousand wagons were used to haul it into position. The central building followed Solomon's pattern: a porch, a central hall and the Holy of Holies. The measurements: 164 feet long, with the porch the same in width and height. The structure was of white stone blocks embellished with gold.

To make the lavish plan – including courtyards in which pilgrims could gather – effective it was necessary to build a huge platform over the original Temple Mount with retaining walls around it. The size of the paved area on which Zerubbabel's – and probably Solomon's – Temple had been built was doubled.

To the west the platform extended into the Tyropoeon (Cheesemakers') Valley. The retaining wall, excavated by Sir Charles Warren (in 1867-70), was sunk into bedrock. A large portion of that wall can still be seen: it is the Western or Wailing Wall. Some of the Herodian blocks are 16.5 feet long by 13 feet wide.

On the other side of the Tyropoeon Valley was the Western Hill on which many lavish homes were built. Edward Robinson (in 1848-52) found the remains of two arches. He believed they were what was left of a great viaduct linking Temple Mount with Western Hill and, therefore, spanning the valley. Since 1968 Benjamin Mazar's excavations have suggested that the arches were part of a grand stairway leading down into the valley. Certainly there is evidence that there was such a stairway. But Josephus Flavius (*Jewish Wars*, XV ix 3) refers to a magnificent royal platform built by Herod on the Western Hill and a viaduct spanning the valley to link it to the temple. Wilson's Arch has also been found to be one of a series of archways supporting a road from the temple platform to the Western Hill.[2]

To the east the retaining walls rose 450 feet from the Kidron Valley. Dame Kathleen Kenyon pointed out that from the south-east corner of Jerusalem's walls Herodian masonry is visible for a distance of 180 metres. Herod's platform 'completely encased' those of Solomon and Zerubbabel. Scarcely a trace of Zerubbabel's temple survives.[3]

Having paid his dues to God, Herod proceeded to pay his dues to Caesar.

To the north of the beautiful temple compound a huge, ugly, functional fort was built. Its size was such that it dominated the temple. Herod named it the Antonia Fortress after Mark Antony.

Beneath the Convent of the Sisters of Zion, excavators working between 1903 and 1904 found a Roman courtyard. The Lithostratos was, until recently, believed to have been the 'Gabbatha' of John 19:13, the courtyard of the Praetorium. As late as 1982 one authority was prepared to go still further; 'the pavement . . . formed Pilate's Hall of Judgement from which Jesus was led to the cross'.[4] Archaeologists from the Hebrew University viewed the Lithostratos as 'the pavement of a forum (a central plaza)'.[5]

But British and American scholars remain unconvinced, pointing out the proximity of the 'pavement' to the two great water cisterns (completely excavated and unquestionably a part of Herod's fort).

In Jerusalem, Herod also built a palace for himself (located inside the present Jaffa Gate). A part of one tower remains.[6]

The city of Caesarea on the coast was another of Herod the Great's achievements. Between 25 and 13BC Herod superintended the construction of a new city and a modern harbour there. He was determined to make use of the very best concepts in civil engineering. A number of piers were constructed for the berthing of ships, together with storage buildings and hostels for seamen. There is still much to be seen at Caesarea, but it is scattered along a mile and a half of shoreline. Some of the huge blocks of limestone, 50 feet by 10 feet in size, remain from the great wall constructed to keep out the sea from the harbour. Today most impressive of all is the aqueduct, completely excavated.

After the death of Herod the Great, Caesarea became the headquarters of Roman governors and remained so from AD6 to AD66. There the apostle Paul met Felix, Festus and Agrippa (Acts 23:23-26:32).

One of the most fascinating discoveries made during the renovation of the amphitheatre is a stone inscription bearing the name of Pontius Pilate.

Two miles west of Old Jericho, where the *Wadi Qelt* opens into the Jordan Valley, Herod built his winter palace. It was excavated in 1949 and is best viewed from the old, original road from Jerusalem to Jericho as it snakes downward through the lunar landscape towards the Jordan Valley.

Only after excavations began in 1973 did it become clear that it was, in fact, a winter palace built in characteristic Herodian style and occupied by Herod and his successors.

In a bare spot, high on the mountains to the east of the Dead

Sea, Herod rebuilt the sinister fortress-palace of Machaerus to provide himself with extra security.

To the west of the Dead Sea on a flat-topped mountain he built a fortress city. Initially Masada had been fortified by the Maccabees. Around this self-sufficient, fortified city there was a sheer drop of 1,300 feet to the western shore of the Dead Sea.

To the northern extremity he built a three-tier palace: a villa on each of the three terraces below the top level of the rock and away from the fierce glare of the sun. Following the fall of Jerusalem in AD70, the Zealots held out in Masada for three years until Roman General Silva, using Jewish slave labour from En Gedi, constructed a vast ramp and stormed the 'impregnable fortress' – to find that everyone, with the exception of a handful of women and children, had committed suicide.

In 27BC Herod commenced extensive building work at Samaria. He built a new city contained within walls two and a half miles long with towers at intervals.

In 4BC, Herod died not long after ordering the murder of the innocents in nearby Bethlehem. He was buried beneath *Herodion. Herodion* was Herod's summer palace built atop an artificially constructed hill in the barren waste to the south of Bethlehem. Excavation work there carried out in 1962 and 1967 revealed a large circular palace.

Herod's Jerusalem contained an amphitheatre, a hippodrome, a theatre, public squares and new paved streets and colonnades that covered acres of ground. Many of them still await the spade of the archaeologist.

At Hebron is a Herodian building almost intact. The great structure built by Herod over the traditional site of the Cave of Machpelah (containing the tombs of Abraham, Sarah, Isaac, Rebekah, Jacob and Leah) has somehow escaped the ravages of centuries of conquerors. Among the reasons for that is that it is sacred to the Muslim, Christian and Jewish religions.

Most of the building on the Jerusalem temple had been completed by 9BC. However, all work was not completed until AD64, just two years before the beginning of the Jewish revolt. Herod's temple was used during the revolt as a fortress by the rebels and hence became a focus of attack by the Romans. By August AD70 all Jerusalem had been conquered by Titus, son of Roman Emperor Vespasian – all *except* the temple. The Zealots refused to surrender. Against the express instructions of Titus, Roman soldiers set fire to the woodwork of the temple buildings and threw a torch into the inner sanctum itself. The fire burned furiously; even the gold melted. The destruction was so complete that, literally, not one stone was left upon another. Exactly, indeed, as Jesus had prophesied (Matthew 24:1, 2).

New Testament accuracy confirmed

The main sites associated with the ministry of Jesus in Galilee, Judaea and the surrounding areas have been positively identified. With regard to the sites of Bethlehem, Nazareth, the Sea of Galilee, Cana, Nain, Capernaum and Chorazin 'there can be no reasonable doubt'.[6]

Much of the Galilean ministry of Jesus centred around Capernaum. Excavations at this once-thriving centre of trade stretch over one mile of the Galilean shore. First to be excavated, and partially restored, was an ancient synagogue. Built of white limestone – in contrast to the native stone, black basalt – and in the Roman style, it was for many years assumed to have been the first-century synagogue mentioned so many times in the four gospels and built at the expense of a Roman centurion (Luke 7:5).

The dating of other synagogues in the Galilean region led archaeologists to doubt the first-century date of the Capernaum synagogue. It is now assumed that in the military campaigns of Vespasian and Titus in Galilee all synagogues were systematically destroyed. However, research done between 1986 and 1987 beneath the existing ruins has provided conclusive evidence that, as might be expected, one synagogue was built over the ruins of another. Hence, while the present visible ruins almost entirely date from the fourth century, they are those of a synagogue built over the site of the first-century synagogue presided over by Jairus and in which Jesus performed certain of his miracles.

Around the shoreline of Galilee, of the twenty settlements (each with a population in excess of 20,000) in existence at the time of Jesus, only one remains. It was built between AD14 and 22 by Herod Antipas and named after the Roman caesar Tiberius. Antipas had it built over an ancient Jewish cemetery. For that reason it was shunned by the devout for much of the first century. Indeed, although it is mentioned in the gospels, there is no evidence that Jesus actually preached there. After the fall of Jerusalem in AD70, however, Tiberias became the main centre of Jewish scholarship.

Among the New Testament writers Luke takes greatest pains in setting the events associated with the life of Jesus and the growth of the early church against a background of secular history. It is perhaps for this reason that the nineteenth-century critics subjected Luke to the most intensive investigations. Destroy the credibility of Luke's writings in his gospel and the book of Acts, and the historicity of the whole of the Testament will be undermined. F. C. Baur of the Tubingen School asserted that statements in Acts 'can only be looked upon as intentional deviations from historic truth'.[7]

Other biblical researchers and archaeologists, most notably Sir William Ramsay, began to do their research on the historical accuracy of Luke's two books, more especially the book of Acts. Ramsay began from a position of extreme scepticism with regard to the biblical record: 'I began with a mind unfavourable to it, for the ingenuity and apparent completeness of the Tubingen theory had at one time quite convinced me.' However, after a detailed and painstaking investigation of the book of Acts and of the topography, antiquities and society of Asia Minor, Ramsay was able to make the following statement: 'It was gradually borne in upon me that in various detail the (biblical) narrative showed marvellous truth. In fact, beginning with the fixed idea that the work was essentially a second-century composition and never relying on its evidence as trustworthy for first-century conditions, I gradually came to find it a useful ally in some obscure and difficult investigations.'[8]

What redirected the thinking of Ramsay, and eventually a whole generation of Bible scholars, was the fact that archaeological investigation demonstrated that the historical, geographical, topographical and political atmosphere of the books of Luke and Acts authenticated in the minutest detail Luke's sound, historical and political sense, as well as his grasp of geography.

The Tubingen School had, in particular, attacked Luke's accuracy in two respects: =1. His dating of the birth of Christ: '*In those days Caesar Augustus issued a decree that a census should be taken of the entire Roman world. (This was the first census that took place while Quirinius was governor of Syria.)*' (Luke 21:1, 2, NIV.) 2. His date for the emergence of John the Baptist: '*In the fifteenth year of the reign of Tiberius Caesar — when Pontius Pilate was governor of Judaea, Herod tetrarch of Galilee, his brother Philip tetrarch of Iturea and Trachonitis and Lysanias tetrarch of Abilene — during the high priesthood of Annas and Caiaphas, the word of God came to John son of Zachariah.*' (Luke 3:1, 2, NIV.)

It had long been accepted by all Bible scholars that when the BC/AD dating system had been worked out centuries after Christ, the dating of the birth of Christ had been miscalculated by between four and six years. Hence the fact that Herod the Great reigned from 37BC to 4BC was a problem to neither school of biblical interpretation. However, F. C. Baur made much of the impossibility of a world-wide census and that the governorship of Syria by Quirinius overlapped with the reign of Herod the Great.

After years of research Ramsay was able to explain the apparent difficulties very clearly. He pointed out that Luke had used the present tense of the verb deliberately and had meant 'that Augustus had ordered enrolments to be regularly taken', that is, that he had laid down the principle of systematic 'enrolment' in the Roman world, not made arrangements for taking one single, world-wide census. He produced detailed records of these repeated 'enrolments' in Egypt. Further, he provided evidence that the enrolments were, generally, separated by fourteen years. He even discovered that the census which necessitated the journey of Mary and Joseph from Nazareth to Bethlehem was probably two years late. The extraordinary circumstances in Palestine and Syria, Ramsay argued, accounted for the delay of the census in Herod's kingdom.[9]

Similarly, Ramsay had an ingenious way of dealing with Baur's assertion that Quirinius was *not* governor of Syria in the year of Christ's birth, 4BC, but that his governorship commenced some years later. Ramsay found that the Greek word translated 'governor' in Luke 2:2 merely implied 'oversight'. He produced inscriptions that proved that Quirinius had 'oversight' over Syria during two separate periods. Professor F. F. Bruce, half a century on, examined Ramsay's evidence. He succeeded in producing more artefacts to substantiate the view that Quirinius was, in fact, the imperial legate in Syria during the final years of the reign of Herod the Great.[10]

The Tubingen attack on the accuracy of Acts ridiculed the idea that '*a severe famine*' '*spread over the entire Roman world . . . during the reign of Claudius*' (Acts 11:27, 28, NIV). Ramsay discovered in the writings of Roman historian Suetonius many references to famine prices under Claudius Caesar. In the writings of Dio Cassius and Tacitus he found references to two famines in Rome, as well as famines elsewhere in the Mediterranean world. Ramsay discovered in *Eusebius* references to a famine in Greece. He discovered an inscription in Asia Minor to a widespread famine in the Roman provinces there during the reign of Claudius. Indeed he found that the imperial reign of Claudius (AD41-54) was marked by a succession of bad harvests which caused serious famines. He linked one such famine with the collection made by Paul on behalf of the Jerusalem church in AD46.

During Paul's first missionary journey he visited Cyprus. In the course of thirty-five years Cyprus had had four different types of Roman government. Displaying acute political awareness, Luke was careful to give the correct title of 'deputy' to a Roman official mentioned in Acts 13:7. That displayed his awareness of the nature of the Roman government in the exact year of Paul's visit. The 'deputy's' name was Sergius Paulus. Among Ramsay's discoveries on Cyprus was an inscription bearing the name of that deputy.

The Asia Minor of Paul's missionary journeys was a jigsaw of provincial frontiers. Ramsay demonstrated that Luke was meticulous in his account, both with regard to geographical and political frontiers. On certain points of detail, Luke's accuracy had been challenged; the archaeological discoveries of Ramsay and his successors have proved Luke, not his nineteenth and twentieth-century detractors, to be correct.

Ramsay concluded his exhaustive examination of the historical data of the book of Acts with these words:

'Luke is a historian of the first rank; not merely are his statements of fact trustworthy; he is possessed of the true historic sense; he fixes his mind on the idea and plan that rules in the evolution of history, and proportions the scale of his treatment to the importance of each incident. He seizes the important and critical events and shows that true nature at greater length, while he touches lightly, or omits entirely, much that was valueless for his purpose. In short, this author should be placed along with the greatest of the historians.'[11]

Not for the first time, the Bible was right – and the critics were wrong.

References:
[1] J. A. Thompson, *The Bible and Archaeology*, third edition, page 290.
[2] Ibid, pages 294, 297.
[3] Kathleen Kenyon, *Archaeology of the Holy Land*, fourth edition, pages 240, 306.
[4] J. A. Thompson, *op cit*, page 298.
[5] Rivka Gonen, *Biblical Holy Places*, page 154.
[6] G. E. Wright and F. V. Wilson, *Westminster Historical Atlas*, cited J. A. Thompson, *op cit*, page 371.
[7] Cited J. A. Thompson, *op cit*, page 385.
[8] W. M. Ramsay, *St Paul the Traveller*, pages 7 *et seq.*
[9] Ibid, pages 4-17, 174-179.
[10] F. F. Bruce, *Are the New Testament Documents Reliable?*, page 85; J. A. Thompson, *op cit*, pages 385-388.
[11] W. M. Ramsay. *The Bearing of Recent Discovery on the Trustworthiness of the New Testament*, page 222.

5

In conclusion

The message of the Book

Taste and see

The Bible is not true because the findings of archaeologists authenticate as fact the details of its narrative. Or because, against the longest odds imaginable, the discovery of ancient manuscripts in the past 200 years or so has demonstrated that its text has not been corrupted by time. Or because, down the centuries, men have been prepared to be burned for translating it, or imprisoned for reading it, or to face forced labour camps for distributing it.

The artefacts of archaeology and the manuscripts of history are merely evidences for faith.

Light *is* light. Darkness *is* darkness. They are not what they are because of chemical tests.

Truth *is* truth.

And so the Bible is self-authenticating. The Bible is the sort of book that a man could not write if he would, and would not write if he could. The content of the Bible is such that men and women, by exposing themselves to it, can discover that it is inspired by God.

The challenge is: Taste! See! Read! Discover! Adventure! And it will not be long before you find you are adventuring with God.

Why was the Bible written?

Before we read a book we may want to know something about the author's reason for writing it.

What is he trying to say? Is he the right person to say it? Does what he says have meaning for the contemporary world?

By now we know that the Bible was written by many different authors over a long period of time. We have been at pains to prove that behind the various authors is a single divine Author with a single unifying theme. We have demonstrated the miraculous ways in which that single Author safeguarded his Book from corruption over the centuries and, right on time, permitted evidence to come to light to lend substance to faith.

But what about that purpose or 'unifying theme'?

Paul sets it out crisply in a letter to Timothy: *'From infancy you have known the holy scriptures, which are able to make you wise for salvation through faith in Christ Jesus. All Scripture is God-breathed and is useful for teaching, rebuking, correcting and training in righteousness, so that the man of God may be thoroughly equipped for every good work.'* (2 Timothy 3:15-17, NIV.)

There we have it. Origin of Book: *'God-breathed.'* Object of Book: *'useful'* for human beings.

First of all we had better examine what is meant by the expression *'God-breathed'*. What *did* God have to do with the Bible?

Then we should examine the ways Paul says it can be *'useful'*.

1. What did God have to do with it? Paul wanted Timothy to know that Scripture was breathed out of the mouth of God. What was breathed out of the mouth of God, the many and various writers wrote or spoke. In other words, God did not dictate the Bible. He inspired the minds of its authors, leaving them to express his inspiration in their own words and thought forms.

Right off we have one reason why the Bible was written: *It was God speaking his mind.* The Bible was a miraculous means, devised by a God of miracles, in order to communicate his mind, his purposes and himself to the children made in his image. The Bible is the Word of God through the words of men. God did not ask human authors to take dictation. He allowed the human authors to express themselves in terms appropriate to their culture. He permitted them to develop their own syntax, vocabulary and literary style. God was speaking through men, and men were speaking from God. The Bible has a double authorship. That is what is implied by '*God-breathed*'.

2. *The Bible's usefulness.* Paul linked three words with the Bible's usefulness: '*salvation*', '*Christ*', and '*faith*'.

So the first purpose of the Bible, Paul tells Timothy, is to instruct his readers about *salvation*. Salvation begins when a man senses his need; as long as he thinks he can manage on his own there will be no salvation. When he senses his sinfulness he will reach out to a Power outside of himself. That 'reaching out' will be 'sin-sorrow' or repentance.

God's central purpose in the Old Testament was to foreshadow the contingency plan to be put into practice to deal with the sin problem.

Sin was condemned. Sin's penalty outlined. Sin's solution prefigured, foreshadowed in a hundred different ways.

And the solution to the sin problem was in the second word Paul emphasised: '*Christ*'. The pages of the Old Testament rustled with the rumour of a Coming One. One who would be, at the same time, 'the mighty God' and 'the suffering servant'. One who, like the lambs offered on the altar, would be 'without blemish', 'holy, harmless, undefiled'. As the penitent confessed his sins over the head of the innocent lamb to be slaughtered, so God would send his own Lamb. The 'Lamb of God' — in all things perfect, without blemish — would die for the sins of the fallen race. The sin problem would be resolved in the death of God's son.

Detailed predictions made (in the Old Testament) centuries before the birth of Jesus Christ were fulfilled in his life, death and resurrection.

The gospel writers presented Christ as the perfect sacrifice for sin. Paul in his letters explained the theology of it all. Jesus was the Representative or Substitute for sinful man when he died on the cross on Calvary. By identification with the dying Saviour, the penitent experienced the death of his sins. Through the Saviour's burial was symbolised the burial of sin. In the resurrection was symbolised the accession of the sinner to a new life through a new birth.

The New Testament's revelation of Christ reaches its climax in the last of the sixty-six books of the Bible. In the Book of

Revelation is represented in symbol the whole plan of salvation from the Fall of the first Adam, through the redemption brought by the second Adam (Jesus), to the final restoration of all things when God's eternal kingdom will be set up at the Second Coming of Jesus.

The third word used by Paul to explain why the Bible was 'useful' for human beings was *faith*.

Elsewhere Paul explained that the Scriptures were '*able to make you wise for salvation through faith in Christ Jesus*'. In short: The central purpose of the Bible is to bring us to Christ who, in turn, is the bringer of salvation. But the object of the Scriptures in pointing us to Christ is not simply to provide us with information about him to enable us to understand and admire him. 'Scripture bears witness to Christ, not in order to satisfy our curiosity but in order to draw from us a response of faith.'[1]

Faith and *trust* are synonyms in the New Testament. The object of Scripture is to represent Jesus as absolutely worthy of our trust, to give us every reason to place implicit faith in him and in his sacrifice for sin.

And how was this all-important gift of faith/trust received by the believer? '*Faith comes from hearing the message, and the message is heard through the word of Christ.*' (Romans 10:17, NIV.)

The central purpose of Scripture: To testify to Jesus Christ in order to evoke faith in him, in order to bring salvation to the believer.

Jesus Christ is the central figure in Scripture. The Old Testament foreshadows him from its beginning to its concluding chapter. The New Testament describes his life, ministry, death and resurrection. And in case anyone could have missed the point, the letters of Paul, John, Peter and James, together with John's book of Revelation, make the significance of the life, death and resurrection of Jesus for the sinner crystal clear. The letter to the Romans, in particular, represents a distillation of New Testament theology.

To the Christian the central purpose of Scripture could be summarised in the words employed by the apostle John to describe the aim of his gospel: '*That you may believe that Jesus is the*

Christ, the Son of God, and that by believing you may have life in his name.' (John 20:31, NIV.)

Reference:
[1] John Stott, *Understanding the Bible* (revised edition), page 22.

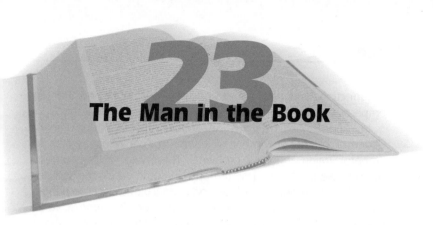

The Man in the Book

Jesus Christ is the central figure of the Bible.

The same nineteenth-century scholars who dated the New Testament books in the second century or later (and have been proved so conclusively wrong) dismissed Jesus as no more than an inspirational preacher. Some even doubted that he had existed at all. Archaeological finds and references to Christ and Christianity in independent (and hostile) sources have made the nineteenth-century view untenable. Oxford's E. P. Thompson in *Jesus and Judaism* recently affirmed: 'The dominant view today seems to be that we can know pretty well what Jesus was out to accomplish, that we can know a lot about what he said, and that these two things make sense within the world of first-century Judaism.'

Jesus in history

The nineteenth-century sceptics who doubted the existence of Jesus and the dating of the rise of Christianity had their views shaken by the discovery of a considerable number of references to Christ and Christianity in the works of Roman historians and in contemporary documents.

In 1889 Dr Rendel Harris found at St Catherine's on Sinai a Syriac translation of a defence of Christianity addressed to the Emperor Antonius Pius by an Athenian philosopher in AD140. It shed a great deal of light on the early history and beliefs of Christianity.

Study of Roman documents proved enlightening. Between the

Resurrection and the conversion of Constantine no Roman emperor was free from anxiety about the 'Christian question'.

In AD108 Gaius Plinius Secundus ('the Younger Pliny'), Governor of the province of Bithynia in Asia Minor, wrote to Emperor Trajan about his problems. There was religious unrest. Temples were virtually deserted and, in some cases, the services discontinued. There was a recession in agriculture because people were no longer buying beasts for sacrifice on the same scale as before. The fault lay with some people called 'Christians' whose loyalty was highly suspect because they refused to offer sacrifices to the god-emperor. He had brought many Christians to trial but had failed to find evidence of criminal activity. All he had been able to accuse them of was 'degraded and extravagant superstition'. They met on a certain day each week to sing hymns to Christ 'as to a god' and to bind themselves on solemn oath to keep the moral law: not to rob or steal, or commit adultery, or defraud. The service was followed by a ritual meal together. Everything was harmless on the surface, but their attitude towards the Emperor, asserted Pliny, made them highly suspect. Pliny, *Correspondence with Trajan*, letters 96 and 97.

In AD112 Cornelius Tacitus was writing a *History of the Rome of the Emperors*. In the imperial reign of Nero there had, he said, been a great fire that had devastated Rome. To take attention from the half-mad Emperor – believed by many to have been the arsonist – the Roman authorities had picked on the Christians as scapegoats. The 'Christians', Tacitus explained for the benefit of his readers, were almost universally unpopular in Rome and suspected of all manner of doubtful, clandestine religious rites. A vast number of Christians had been arrested. The excruciating tortures to which they had been subjected and the grisly deaths they had died swung Roman opinion round in their favour.

Tacitus made it clear that *he* did not believe the Christians to have been the true incendiaries. However, their founder had been a criminal who had been executed by Pontius Pilate, procurator of Judaea, some thirty years earlier.

The death of the ringleader, said Tacitus, had not stopped the 'pestilent superstition', but had given impetus to its growth. By the time Tacitus wrote, its adherents were an 'immense multitude'.

Referring to Tacitus, Professor C. H. Dodd has said, 'Here at last, from a reputable Roman historian, we have an account of the beginnings of Christianity in the late twenties or early thirties of the first century.'[1]

Both Pliny and Tacitus, sources hostile to Christianity, provide independent corroboration of its early growth and development. So, ironically, does the Jewish *Talmud*.[2] In the era of division and dissension in the first half of the first century, says the *Talmud*, 'they hanged Jesus of Nazareth on the Eve of Passover'. He had been, apparently, 'leading Israel astray'.

There are other contemporary or near contemporary sources which provide more corroborative evidence of the existence of Jesus and (indirectly) the impact of his resurrection felt in the wild-fire growth of the Christian Church. Among them, Josephus Flavius (a Jewish historian who was a contemporary of Jesus and his disciples), Lucian of Samosata (a second-century satirist), Suetonius (an early second-century Roman historian), as well as the writings of the Church fathers, including Polycarp, Eusebius, Irenaeus, Ignatius, Justin, Origen, Tertullian and others. F. F. Bruce brought together all the ancient documents and published them in his *Jesus and Christian Origins Outside the New Testament*.

In the fifteenth edition of *Encyclopaedia Britannica*, volume 3, page 145, after a summary of the references to Christ in primary source material outside the New Testament, the authors conclude:

'These independent accounts prove that in ancient times even the opponents of Christianity never doubted the historicity of Jesus, which was disputed for the first time and on inadequate grounds by several authors at the end of the eighteenth, during the nineteenth and at the beginning of the twentieth centuries.'

The Jesus of the gospels

Of course, the main source of information about Jesus is in the four gospels.

Like the rest of Scripture, the gospels are self-authenticating, as we have endeavoured to demonstrate. A good place to start reading the Bible is with the gospel of Mark. Mark was the amanuensis of Peter. How fascinating, then, to find that it is Mark's gospel that sets Peter in the worst light! Mark's candour is disarming. Developments we might consider important are given scant treatment. Events are described in detail which no writer could possibly have invented.

There are many details in the four gospel accounts that would have been excluded from a secular, contemporary biography. John the Baptist, at one point, is described as having his doubts regarding the authenticity of Jesus. He sent a message: '*Are you the one who was to come, or should we expect someone else?*' Like a good reporter the apostle John reports the negative audience-reaction to the sermon recorded in John 6 (verses 41, 42, 43, 52, 60, 61). Jesus' loss of a mass following is candidly reported (John 6:66). Matthew records that in his home town Jesus did not work many miracles (Matthew 13:58). Luke is prepared to report the words of unbelievers who regard Christianity as a superstition (Acts 25:18, 19).

Short of embellishing the reputation of Jesus, again and again the gospel writers provide us with examples showing that accurate reportage was more important than making a good impression. In his letters Paul showed the same disinclination to embellish his own reputation. In the first chapter of his letter to the Galatians he confessed to having been a blasphemer and a persecutor. The autobiographical details he provides in his letter to the Philippians chapter 3 verses 4 and 10 are far from flattering. Not without humour, he sets out the ridiculous arrogance of his former days and confesses that the religion he had espoused with such passion had been valueless; that his whole life had been value-less – apart from the resurrection power of Jesus.

The gospel writers set out bluntly the claims of Jesus to be the Christ, the Messiah, God's Son. Jesus is the only Man who ever lived who claimed to be God and yet was judged sane by his wisest contemporaries. Confucius did not claim to be God, nor Zoroaster, nor Buddha, nor Muhammad. They had too much regard for their credibility. C. S. Lewis was correct with regard to the claims of Jesus. He said that, having made such claims, Jesus had to be mad, bad – or God. No one, apparently, is suggesting that he was mad or bad. True enough, some have made the claim that he was 'simply a great teacher'. But how could he have been – making such claims? He did not leave us that option. He was mad, or bad or . . .

Christ in both Old and New Testaments

Scores of prophecies in the Old Testament were fulfilled by the Jesus of the New Testament. Christ makes the unity between the two testaments. All sixty-six books enshrine him. The chief characters, institutions and histories prefigure him.

The Cross was the Tree of Life in the midst of the desolation of Earth; it had been prefigured in Eden. In John's gospel it is clear that Christ saw in himself the fulfilment of Jacob's ladder, of the manna that fed Israel in the wilderness, of the rock that was smitten to provide water, of the pillar of fire that went before the people, of the uplifted serpent that brought healing.

In Eden, Adam, the head of the race, fell asleep so that a bride could be taken from his side. On the Cross, Jesus, the second Adam, slept the sleep of death; and, during that sleep, a spear opened his side to bring forth his bride, the Church. (Throughout the New Testament the Church is symbolised as a bride.)

And Adam is by no means the only Old Testament character to prefigure Christ. There is Joseph, his father's most beloved son, betrayed by his brethren for pieces of silver. There is Moses the lawgiver, the deliverer, who left a palace to redeem his people, and was willing to be blotted out for the sins of his people. There is David the warrior who never lost a battle when leading God's people and whose name means 'Beloved', who was born in Bethlehem, and who, as a young man, overcame the giant of evil.

From first to last in Scripture it is difficult to escape its central figure: Jesus Christ. Three hundred and thirty-two distinct Old Testament prophecies were literally fulfilled in the person of Jesus. The mathematical probability of all those prophecies being fulfilled in one person is one over eighty-four with ninety-seven zeros.

His teaching

No single person has so changed the course of history, has been so loved and so despised, so hated and so adored, has so turned the bad into the good, the ugly into the beautiful – as Jesus of Nazareth.

Everywhere he went people murmured, 'What sort of man is this? Who is this?' The more we look at the person of Jesus the more we find it impossible to link him with all the other religious leaders who have emerged in the course of history.

The people who heard Jesus caught their breath. He spoke with astonishing authority. When he tackled the great questions of life and death and God and man he spoke with final, unquestionable authority. And yet he was manifestly humble, meek, and lowly of heart.

He worked with the same authority with which he spoke. Sickness disappeared in his presence. Leprosy faded away. Demons shrieked and scrambled. Death gave up its claimed victims. A mob in Nazareth intent on pushing him over a precipice fell back at his commanding presence. The very Temple Guard sent to arrest him in Gethsemane at first fell back in confusion; even *there*, even *then*, he was in command of the situation.

Jesus gathered around him the most extraordinary bunch of people. Among them were uneducated fishermen, patriotic freedom fighters, a traitor-to-be; men who were impulsive, weak, pessimistic, jealous, in all senses fallible. He saw potential in them that was only fully realised after his death and resurrection. But even in his lifetime there were minor miracles in their relationships. If Simon the Zealot had met Matthew the tax collector anywhere but in the presence of Jesus he would have cut his throat. Men normally full of hate could learn to love in the presence of Jesus.

The breathtaking thing about Jesus is not just his miracles or his preaching: but his sheer character. He was anything but a professional holy man, all pious and ascetic. In fact he was so ordinary, so much like anyone else, that the establishment figures of his day were offended when he flouted some of their religious customs. Some said, 'We can't accept *him* as Messiah. Isn't he the carpenter's son? Not only that; he mixes with sinners and ordinary folk. He never turns anyone away.' If we knew nothing about Jesus except what was said of him by his opponents, he would still appear as the most lovable of beings ever to walk the surface of this planet.

To everyone he showed love; there were no exceptions. The lonely, the despised, the outcast, the prostitute, the thief, the leper: he loved everybody. He gave respect and dignity to women who were despised and misused. More than anyone else in history he established the principle of the sanctity of human life. Jesus gave both women and children a greatly improved status.

His teaching was direct, sometimes unnervingly so. He unerringly exposed the selfish, greedy, proud, hypocritical, ambitious men for what they really were – and are. He pointed them to an entirely new way of living. Upset their value systems. He began the Sermon on the Mount: 'Blessed are the poor in spirit . . . ; blessed are the meek. . . .' But the world of his day, like ours, said: Look after Number One! Act confident! Stick up for your rights! Get your own back! Don't get involved! Keep out of trouble! Who cares anyway?

By contrast the message of Jesus was: Admit your need of God. Confess your sin-sorrow. Surrender your life to God. He is either Lord *of* all, or he's not Lord *at* all! Seek first his kingdom, his righteousness. You're hurting? Forgive those who have hurt you! Make peace on Earth! Trust God in every situation.

And, with the perspective of history, who can say that Jesus was wrong? His teaching meets the deepest cries and needs of men and women of all cultures, of all ages. He is the light in our darkness; the purpose in an otherwise purposeless life; the meaning in an otherwise meaningless existence.

The Cross

Christ is the central figure in Scripture.

The Cross is its central symbol. All Scripture and (according to Scripture) all history lie beneath its shadow.

The very shape of the Cross suggests the length, breadth and height of the love of God. Men may reject an angry God. But how can they reject a God who, even at the point of their rejection, leans forward in entreaty?

The week ending in his crucifixion is the great emphasis of all four gospels. Only one day in every 350 in the life of Jesus is even referred to in the accounts of Matthew, Mark, Luke and John. But the record of the events of the last seven days takes up one-third of the gospel account.

Why? Because at the Cross was the clearest depiction of the heart and mind of God. The Cross tells us about man and about God, about good and about evil, about Earth and about Heaven. It tells us about holiness, and law, and righteousness, and forgiveness, and mercy, and peace and love.

In the mystery of the Cross all other mysteries are made plain. The Cross could be the darkest spot in the history of existence; but when we see it as a revelation of God it becomes the searchlight by which we can penetrate the thickest gloom and the darkest tragedy. The Cross is the main beam lighting the way to eternity.

There is the reason why God can forgive sin. *There* is the reason why his law must be viewed as eternal. *There* is viewed the infinite depths of evil. And *there* the scale of heaven's righteousness and the breadth of heaven's mercy. There alone: the motivation to faith, hope and love. *There* is the difference between Christianity and other religions and philosophies. Only Christianity can evoke faith, hope and love. Only those motivations can change a messed-up life. Only the Cross can do it. It's not enough to *know* what's right. What men need is not just information as to what they should do. It's the motivation to do it.

And on Bad Friday – the day of the Cross – what would we have seen?

The Prisoner with a crown made of the long-thorned briar crushed savagely down on his brow.

A lacerated back. A flagellum was a whip tipped with nails and bits of bone, and it had been wielded by soldiers with arms like shot-putters. The hideous shape of the Cross upon the ground. Huge Roman nails, square in section, hammered through the wrists and feet of the Prisoner.

The entire hideous instrument of torture and execution, with the Prisoner upon it hoisted in the air and savagely jolted down into the place prepared.

The cries. The intense, insupportable agony, caused by the incomplete severing of the median nerves by the nails through the wrists, vibrating through the arm to explode in the brain at every movement . . . endlessly twisting, seeking relief from that onslaught on the senses. . . .

And, at length, the loud voice of a strong man crying, '*It is finished.*'

It was 3pm on the day of the Passover. On that day for fifteen centuries, and at that hour, Israel had slain her Passover lamb. Jesus died at Passover time: at the very month, day and hour of the Passover lamb. Long before the Passover lamb had saved the firstborn of Israel. On Bad Friday the firstborn of heaven became the Passover Lamb through whom the world could find its redemption.

And there is the point and the purpose of Scripture.

Through the Cross of Christ God is saying to man: That is where you ought to be. Jesus, my Son, hangs there in your place. His tragedy is the tragedy of your life. You are the rebel who should be hanged on the gallows. But stay; here is your ladder up to heaven. This is the place of your salvation. You must meet me at the Cross by identifying with the One on the Cross. It is by this identification that I, God, can meet you in him, saying to you as I say to him: 'My beloved son'.

His brow thorn-crushed for the wrong thoughts your mind has harboured. His hands nail-pierced for the wrong things your hands have done. His feet spiked through for the wandering paths your feet have trod.

We were there, our upturned faces contorted with hate and scorn, our characters warped by sin. *We* swung the hammer. *We* drove the nails. *We* were the crucifiers. His words, '*Father, forgive them,*' were for our hearing, and our acceptance.

Acceptance by faith. The faith that comes through hearing, and the hearing that comes through the Word of God.

References:
[1] C. H. Dodd, *The Founder of Christianity*, page 17.
[2] Babylonian *Talmud*. Tractate *Sanhedrin*, 436.

Index